Life at Daniel's Place

Also by Alice J. Wisler

Slices of Sunlight

Down the Cereal Aisle

Rain Song

How Sweet It Is

Hatteras Girl

A Wedding Invitation

Still Life in Shadows

Under the Silk Hibiscus

Getting Out of Bed in the Morning

Memories Around the Table

The Mom Spa Journal

Life at Daniel's Place

How the cemetery became a sanctuary
of discovery and gratitude

Alice J. Wisler

Life at Daniel's Place
Copyright © 2023
Alice J. Wisler

Edited by Megan Tatreau and RJW
Cover photo by the author

Published by Daniel's House Publications
Durham, North Carolina, USA

Print copy - ISBN: 978-09676740-6-3

For
Rachel, Ben, and Liz

What we have once enjoyed we can never lose. All that we love deeply becomes a part of us.

~ Helen Keller, *We Bereaved*

Teach us to number our days, that we may gain a heart of wisdom.

~ Psalm 90:12

~*~
Prologue
2020

Weeks after the governor shut down North Carolina
due to the coronavirus pandemic, I put on a pair of
tennis shoes. It was a Sunday in April, yet my
church held no services. Since I couldn't go there to
worship, I drove across town to Markham Memorial
Gardens. People feared the virus, but fear was
nowhere on the rolling lawn dotted with grave
markers and tall Carolina pines. *The dead can't get
Covid. And I can't get the illness from them.* As I
drove, I smiled at my dark humor.

But my humor evaporated once I faced the white
wooden fence at the entrance. My eyes blurred with
tears. The tears, which I'm a fanatic about labeling,
were not tears of sorrow, hurt, or pain. They were
those special tears cried when we know someone
has cared for, looked after, and loved us, even when
we didn't realize what was happening. My spirit had

come to this place for safety, but not from Covid or our country's looming troubles. Long before news of the virus and the shutdown, this corner of the world had become my secure haven and respite.

As I walked the circular driveway, passing the familiar gravestones and landmarks, flashbacks played through my mind. Here, I had once wanted to die, before my healing had begun.

Four years into my grief, I was invited to facilitate a writing workshop. Sascha, a poet and bereaved mother who had lost both her children—the youngest to drowning and the oldest to suicide—asked me to fill in for her at a conference in Denver, Colorado. She was ill and needed a substitute. I was instructed to share how beneficial writing from heartache is. As I stood at the podium before forty bereaved parents, I knew writing helped me. But did others find it therapeutic? I introduced some writing prompts and was pleased when parents stood to read their poetry in memory of their son or daughter.

After I made it through the workshop—where I hoped no one had noticed my insecurity from being a novice—one of the event volunteers approached me. I thought she was trying to make me feel good when she said, "Alice, there was a lot of healing going on in that room." I had no idea what a room of healing looked like.

Decades later, I know. I know how a grassy landscape of remorse becomes a sanctuary of discovery and gratitude. I know how God takes our most profound agony and replaces it with his joy. I know how pouring pain onto paper transforms pent-up anguish into hope. I have experienced how a mother lacking confidence dared to seek fulfillment. This did not happen over weeks; it took years.

The cemetery welcomed me that Sunday in April. True, the dead were still silent; they could no longer share their opinion, ponder, or rush to be anywhere. For them, what was done was done; it was over. As for me, I still had a course to run— peace to absorb, ideas to wrestle with, lessons to invite, and healing to embrace. Gratitude for the quiet landscape rich with my history filled me; I started to sing. I belted out one of my favorite hymns, repeating the first verse six times because that was the only verse I knew from heart. "Our God, our help in ages past, our hope for years to come, our shelter from the stormy blast, and our eternal home."

And that is another pleasure of being at the cemetery: the dead don't complain.

~*~
One
1997

The first time I saw my son Daniel's gravestone, I knew I'd made a mistake.

I hadn't surveyed the entire cemetery; I hadn't walked down the slope toward the chalky Jesus statue and looked at every grave between. But I did see that the flat cuts of granite neighboring my son's were all larger. Even Audrey, who had lived one day, had a wide stone with a bronze heart stretched across it. A metal flower container emerged from the middle of that heart. The container held artificial crimson flowers with sunny centers. Daniel had no vase attached to his gravestone. His resting place was big enough to hold only the inscribed words:

Daniel P. Wisler
Aug. 25, 1992 - Feb. 2, 1997
Our Darling Boy.

After Daniel's death, my husband, David, and I went to the funeral home to identify our child's body. Inside a small office seated across from the director, we were instructed to pick out Daniel's gravestone from a catalogue. My eyes were bloodshot and sore. I wanted the pounding in my head to stop. I wanted time to rewind. I wanted my son back. I pointed to a photo of one of the markers, not realizing it was the smallest size available.

When the funeral home called to say the marker had been laid, we got in the van to make the drive to the cemetery. As David stood beside me in silence, we viewed the flat stone that covered our son's urn. I expected my husband to say something like, "I guess we should have bought a bigger gravestone. I would have, but you're frugal." But he said nothing, and I was grateful I didn't have to make an excuse for the selection of a 12x12-inch marker.

The aroma of cut grass saturated the air. Once, I had been the type to breathe in the scent of spring's freshly-mowed grass and let it fill my lungs while anticipation of summer plans danced through my head.

But on that day, every scent I associated with spring felt like an insult. Spring had come with her beauty, but it was too much color and life. Spring danced like she couldn't get enough of herself, like she knew she was a shimmering goddess. And I had a reason to be at the cemetery.

Bending down, I ran an index finger over the name David and I had given our son: Daniel. Daniel and the lion's den. Brave Daniel. We didn't cite Maurice Sendak, but he was the reason for the three words on the epitaph: *Our Darling Boy*. We'd taken those words from the author's book, *Pierre*, a story Daniel had memorized during his monthly hospital stays where he was injected with drugs to shrink his tumor.

The wind picked up, and the bouquets of real and fake flowers swayed on grave tops. Some containers were filled with plastic poinsettias, their red petals weathered from the sun and rain. Every surrounding grave had a vase mounted to its surface. The only thing that moved on Daniel's grave marker was a clump of dried grass.

"I'm not the type to bring flowers," I told David. "I'm not going to become one of those Sunday afternoon grave visitors." There were no memories of Daniel at this burial ground. His memories were at home, where he'd played with his dinosaurs, Tonka trucks, and siblings. "I can't keep up with driving across town to put flowers here," I said. "And withered flowers will make it look like we don't care." But deep down, I wondered if, even without dried flowers, people might think we really didn't care. We had chosen a marker smaller in length and width than many men's shoe sizes.

We were quiet for a moment, standing with our thoughts.

Then David said, "We miss you, Little Buddy."

I looked away from Daniel's name and into the blue sky filled with plump cumulus clouds. *I'll do big things in your memory. I'll make up for this tiny square.* The writer's voice inside me aimed for what she felt was the highest level of *big things.* She whispered, "I'll share you with the world. I'll write a book."

While our six-year-old, Rachel, had accepted an invitation to play at a neighbor's house instead of joining us, Ben had happily accompanied us to the cemetery. He was a toddler and had no choice. As David and I hovered over Daniel's resting place, Ben was busy taking flowers from one grave and placing them on another. David chased after him, and then I did, too. We hoped we had replaced the correct roses, poinsettias, and sunflowers on the proper graves, but how could we know for sure? Parents in my bereavement group told of how trinkets left for their deceased were either vandalized or stolen. Wait until I told them what I had seen!

The last time I came to the cemetery, the only other time I'd been here, was for the graveside service, when there was a precision-cut hole in the ground. I'd wanted the dirt to reach up and grab my ankles and pull me under. I wouldn't have screamed or fought. I would have gone gracefully, or at least as gracefully as a six-month-pregnant woman can when wearing heels and a dress.

The message filling the cloudy sky then was the same as the message now: *It looks like you're gonna have to figure out how to adapt to this broken life and find a purpose for the pain.*

~*~

Loneliness filled our home on Rolling Meadows Drive. We would never hear Daniel's laughter or his lunchtime prayer again. "Thank you for my food, and thank you for my mommy."

Friends and neighbors listened as I went over all the scenarios that had led to Daniel's demise. I ached, and they appeared to ache along with me. And then, the inevitable happened. The conversations were no longer about Daniel. Someone talked about being cut off in traffic. Another friend was disgruntled about her broken dishwasher. A neighbor showed off her new puppy. So much of what was said around me seemed trivial compared to Daniel's death. How could these topics replace the need I held to focus on my daily feelings of loss and pain?

Life moved on, day after day. Time slipped into the future, and, while it was normal for that to happen, I was disinterested. I opened my journal and wrote about yearning, sorrow, and the continual fear the joy of a belly laugh and my glass-half-full outlook on life were gone.

In the children's book, *Pierre*, it takes being swallowed by a lion for Pierre to trade his I don't care repetitive response with "I care!" Caring is the moral Sendak wanted his readers to embrace. Caring is essential. When you live in an atmosphere of disinterest, you fade.

I read C.S Lewis' book, *A Grief Observed*, and said, "I could have written these words." His sentences resonated, so I read them again and again: *No one ever told me that grief felt so like fear. I am not afraid, but the sensation is like being afraid. At other times it feels like being mildly drunk, or concussed. There is a sort of invisible blanket between the world and me. I find it hard to take in what anyone says. Or perhaps, hard to want to take it in. It is so uninteresting.*

A friend from childhood called, and, as she talked about her family's upcoming visit to Japan, my mind cried out, I don't care! I didn't say those words, but I wanted to end the call. We'd had tickets for a trip to Japan last June, which got canceled when Daniel was diagnosed. Then, to our surprise, Daniel selected Japan for his Make-a-Wish trip. Our family was supposed to go to Japan. Why couldn't we have had that trip and the memories of it to savor? When our conversation ended and we said goodbye, I hung up the phone and collapsed in tears. God didn't love me. God cared about my friend's happiness, but he had abandoned me, David, Rachel, and Ben.

At this rate, I was headed toward becoming a faithless, cynical, ornery woman. In four years, when I reached forty, I'd probably have tossed aside all social graces and be shouting, "I don't care!" every chance I got.

That probability was on my growing list of fears.

One of the deeper fears that stole my sleep was how I'd get through August 25—Daniel's birthday—without him. I *did* care how I would accomplish that.

~*~

Two

Local firemen came to Daniel's fourth birthday. One of them—we knew him from our church— suggested arriving in a shiny red fire truck and bringing red plastic hats for the children on the afternoon of the party. I took photos of the occasion; one shows a pensive Daniel in the truck, uncertain about putting the hat he was given over his bald head.

For months, I grappled with what I could do to make Daniel's birthday without him stand out and be extraordinary. I pondered as I nursed Elizabeth— our newest baby—born just three months after Daniel died. I watched the older two, Rachel and Ben, play with toys Daniel had once enjoyed. How did parents survive a birth date without their son or daughter? How did they get through the twenty-four hours of a day that should celebrate a child growing a year older, knowing this date would never be the same again? There would be no asking Daniel whether he'd like to have spaghetti, curry with rice, egg rolls, or Cocoa Puffs for his birthday meal.

But we had family and friends who had known and cared for Daniel. David and I decided we would make it a day to have them join us and remember a little boy who once ate dirt after knocking over a houseplant and who liked to give away stickers from his hospital bed. We'd have the significant event at the cemetery. That was a plus for me, because I wouldn't have to clean the house, and, with the spaciousness of the cemetery, there would be room for dozens of guests.

Days after Daniel's funeral, my parents had flown back to their missionary work in Japan, so they were unable to attend. I would take pictures to send them of this strange but loving event and place a few in the memorial photo album Rachel and I had started together. At the kitchen table, my eldest and I had cropped photos, stuck them onto pages, and written captions. We named one section—*The Daniel Who Made Us Laugh and Laugh and Laugh*—and included dozens of pictures that showed a boy who was the epitome of humor. There was a picture of Daniel trying on a pair of my maternity pants, and one where he and his friend, Sophie, had gotten into my make-up and smeared red lipstick on their faces. The one with Daniel, Rachel, and my brother, Vince, had both Rachel and Daniel in sunglasses. Daniel's were too big for his face, and in order to keep them seated on his nose, he had to lift his face and stand like a statue.

Markham Memorial Gardens is a secluded park-type location off Farrington Road, sandwiched between Orange and Durham counties. The cemetery is surrounded by trees—large oaks, pines, and junipers—and filled with grassy green slopes decorated with graves. In the hospital, I hadn't wanted to discuss burial or a funeral. In fact, I had banned all death-related talk from Daniel's room.

"He might be comatose," I said to David and Dad, "but he might also be able to hear us. I don't want him to have to listen to talk about his burial and funeral. He *is* still alive."

David got it, and so did Dad.

During Daniel's last days, while I was praying for a miracle, reminding God he had once parted the Red Sea, Dad worked on burial arrangements. With the help of Daniel's pediatric oncologist, Dr. Art, and the phone book, he sorted out the logistics for Daniel's burial.

Mom said, "Dad thinks it's important to have a place to be remembered."

At the time, I didn't realize I would be in debt to my father. He did what I could not do.

~*~

On the evening of the 25th, cars and vans were parked on the circular driveway by Daniel's grave. I'd ordered balloons from Party City and crammed them into our van, the same one where Daniel had sat in the middle row, putting stickers along the window.

As guests arrived, we passed out card stock, markers, pens, and Winnie-the-Pooh, Mickey Mouse, and Toy Story stickers for them to use to decorate and write messages. People sat on the grass; some stood and used their vehicles as backer boards to write notes. We gave each person a helium balloon, and then attached the card stock messages to the balloon strings. We gathered in a circle away from the trees, so there would be a clear path for the balloons to sail into the sky.

When I gave the go-ahead to let the balloons go, it was with the words, "Happy birthday, Daniel." Balloons released, and, one by one, they bounced into the air. Each took its own course. A red one skirted to the left and then right, then centered itself as though waiting on help from the wind to take it on its journey.

I didn't want to let mine go. I wanted to hold onto the string and close my eyes and then click my heels like Dorothy in the *Wizard of Oz* and be back to a day where Daniel was. I'd take a day in the hospital or a day at home doing nothing but just being beside Daniel, breathing in his medicinal scent. Letting my balloon go meant he was really gone. No mama writes a message for her son and affixes it to a balloon string if her son is alive.

I couldn't just stand there holding on, so I relaxed my fingers as the inevitable happened. The string slipped from my hand. I think my heart broke again; I think I heard it yelp. Buoyed by the air, my balloon joined the others and sailed forward and upward, embarking on its journey away from me.

Three dozen red, blue, gold, and green spheres traveled into the blue August sky. All of us watched, hands shading our eyes, squinting into the sun to view the display of color. Soon, what had once been a round object in my hands was just a speck. We kept our necks craned giraffe-like, poised on the grassy knoll.

"I can still see them," said my friend Teresa, whose son, Jordan, had been Daniel's friend.

"There's one trailing along by the cloud," said Caleb's mom, my friend Susan, who was known for loving each of my children. Caleb and Daniel were born the same year; we called them the '92 Boys. Susan's husband had another name for the two— The Demolition Team—because they had once rearranged furniture in search of a plastic Batman.

The balloons all reached heaven, of course. Rachel's eight-year-old friend Avery told Rachel and me days before the party that balloons don't make it to heaven. I could see the disappointment in Rachel's eyes. Rachel and I had planned Daniel's birthday with every detail we could think of. This friend was not going to ruin things for my daughter.

"Avery," I said. "On Daniel's birthday, all the balloons will make it to heaven."

"But you know that isn't possible. You see, that can't happen because they get stuck in electric lines and pop. Or, you see, a bird comes along and—"

"Every balloon." I used my stern voice, reserved for other parents' children. I'd used it on a set of neighbor kids who thought whacking a baseball bat against a tree multiple times was acceptable behavior. "Every one of them will make it to heaven." I kept my eyes steady on hers. I didn't blink. "Okay?"

Avery looked down. I almost felt bad. If she burst into tears, what would I do? "I guess so," she muttered.

"That's right. Balloons go to heaven." Of course, no biblical verse states this, but theology was not my strong suit the last week of August.

Avery learned that day that it's not wise to be logical when it comes to mamas, birthdays of dead children, siblings who miss their brother, and the tribute of balloons.

I learned I could be ferocious when protecting my young. Grief, like a sip of strong Scotch, makes you bold. That is a fact. Too much boldness, like too much drink, can make you fall into crazy and destructive territory. There is a fine line.

At Daniel's Place, we served pizza and angel food cupcakes covered with Betty Crocker rainbow frosting and piped with the words: *We Miss You Daniel*, one letter per cupcake. We sliced a watermelon into large, red, ripe slices. As guests picked up their food from a folding table we'd set up on the grass, I thought this would be a lovely event if Daniel were here. He would enjoy this.

After everyone went home, I stood by the tiniest grave at the cemetery, the one that belonged to me. It would soon be over, this strange day, this birthday without the birthday boy. Before the event, I'd asked friends to bring their written memories of Daniel. I'd bought a three-ring maroon binder and secured the pages inside it, a tribute to Daniel's life. Since he had lived only four years, I feared the stories about him would be forgotten. But now they were contained on paper. They were tangible, collected, and I'd always have them as long as I didn't misplace them.

I breathed in the evening air and brushed a finger across Daniel's marker. "What do you do in heaven?" I whispered. The kids and David were ready to pack up the van and head home. I heard their chatter behind me, but I had one more question. Looking into the sky, I asked, "Daniel, do you ever think of me?"

~*~
Three

The first day of Daniel's life was a Wednesday. I woke at four in the morning to blessed contractions and nudged David. "Teo is coming!" Teo was our nickname for the baby in the womb. We'd called him Teo long before we came up with real name possibilities—ones I liked that David didn't and vice versa. Naming a baby isn't cute or easy; it can be exhausting.

When the ultrasound revealed this baby was male, I said, "How about Daniel Paul?" Although David had nixed using his middle name for our son's middle name, he said, "Okay." Later, I asked him why he gave in. "The way you said it was so cute."

"It's finally happening," David said, as he sat on the edge of the bed in his summer pajamas. "You aren't going to be pregnant forever."

Teo had been seated on my sciatic nerve for ten days and was four days late. When I'd been a day late, David, two-year-old Rachel, and I went to the

17

State Fairgrounds' flea market for the sole purpose of me walking the baby out.

"When are you due?" a vendor selling furniture and knick-knacks asked. She smiled like middle-aged strangers do at pregnant women—tender, kind, sympathetic.

"Yesterday," I said.

"Walk," she instructed.

"I have." I'd walked as much as possible when sciatica pinched at every step. I didn't tell her about sciatica; I just smiled and wobbled toward David and Rachel, who were looking through a box of comic books for sale.

On the morning of August 25, I loved every contraction. I got out of bed while David made his way to the bathroom. His mom had come from South Carolina to care for us. Before she woke, we'd eaten raisin toast with butter, and had packed a bag for the hospital. Thankfully, Rachel stayed asleep in her bedroom, even though in our excitement, we forgot to whisper.

After David took a picture of me by the front door with my large belly, we were off to the hospital. We stopped along the way to get gas and, at the convenience store, bought purple candy called Alexander the Grape, just because we liked the name. David picked up a word search book. This was our second time having a baby; we knew it'd be a long day.

Once situated at the hospital, David asked for a memo pad and recorded the timing of the contractions and an account of the day. When the contractions sent me into heavy breathing, he put his pen down but knew not to rub my back or hold my hand. I wanted him with me but didn't want any physical contact. A young, skinny intern entered and massaged my shoulder. She cooed, "You are doing great, Mrs. Wisler. So good, Mrs. Wisler." I felt David bristle and knew he was afraid I might shove her onto the floor.

When the doctor checked my uterus and told me it was time to push, I grunted and groaned and thought my body would explode. Three more hard pushes and out came this baby. Slippery, fleshy, bald.

The nurse weighed him and laughed.

The doctor leaned over to look at the scale. "Ten pounds, seven and a half ounces," he announced before she could. "He'll be walking out of here!"

Minutes later, a nurse with red hair and a broad smile entered to see this big baby. She'd been in the delivery room five minutes when another came in.

The second nurse looked at Daniel, who was warm against my chest. "Congratulations! How are you feeling?"

"She delivered this baby with just a small tearing," said the doctor.

"And no epidural." My husband smiled at me.

We were asked if Daniel could be on TV, some program filmed at the hospital about smart moms and healthy babies. He'd be filmed in the hospital bassinet in the background while two hostesses discussed a segment of the show. I signed the papers in agreement and jokingly said this could be the beginning of his film career. Mandy, a friend in our neighborhood, had also had a baby boy. She had a scheduled C-section, so while I was pushing, Mandy was done and drinking a cup of coffee in her room. Her newborn was included on this show. Both babies slept through their first-ever screen appearance.

That night, in the hospital room alone with Daniel, while the news on TV showed the catastrophe in Florida from Hurricane Andrew's fury, I breathed in my newborn's scent and smiled into his eyes. "Thank you for being a boy. Thank you, thank you. Now I can hang up those maternity clothes for good."

I didn't know how unpredictable life could be or how humans plan and think we are wise and hold the reins to control. Even though I was convinced we were not going to have any more children, shortly after Daniel turned three, another baby entered our lives. Benjamin was a placid and sweet baby, and I couldn't imagine life without him. Rachel and Daniel enjoyed his company. Our family—now five—although not planned by us, was a blessing. Yet, David and I knew we had to make sure I didn't get pregnant again. David decided to have a vasectomy, saving me from having my tubes tied. His procedure was done, and, six weeks later, David went for a follow-up visit. All looked fine. No more babies for the Wislers.

Four months into Daniel's treatments, I wondered why I felt pregnant. David called from the urologist to tell me I was carrying our fourth. After slight dismay, I turned positive. We'd be *The Wisler Six*. Daniel would be done with treatments by the time his sibling arrived. Four children—I liked even numbers—it would be fun! But Daniel would leave before his youngest sister had a chance to say hello.

~*~

As the day gave into darkness, we drove home. Memories of Daniel's birth flickered like distant stars. At home, we stored the leftover cupcakes and pizza. David and I got the kids ready for bed. Relief washed over me. Soon this day would end, and, if I didn't die in the next three hours, I would have survived Daniel's first birthday without him.

Next, I'd have to deal with Christmas, but that was four months away. There was still plenty of time for David and me to figure out our plans for that day.

And perhaps, the Second Coming would take place before then, and I wouldn't have to face December 25 at all.

~*~
Four

When we entered the life of living with a child with childhood cancer, I expected Daniel's healing. I thought his cancer was just a test to strengthen our dependence on God and draw us closer to him. The oncologists shared Daniel's protocol with us— monthly hospital stays for chemotherapy, surgeries, scans, and radiation. We would get through this life disruption that started with a lump.

~*~

The last day of April 1996 was when the growth decided to make itself known. It was like it could no longer hide and had been permitted to enter center stage.

After dropping Rachel off at kindergarten that morning, with the dogwood and azaleas rejuvenating neighboring lawns, Daniel, Benjamin, and I went to the new McDonald's on Glenwood in Raleigh for breakfast. Daniel loved the pancakes and syrup. Playing in the ball pit at the indoor playground was also fun for him.

I pulled into the parking lot and turned to smile at my boys. My heart filled with love and all that gooey stuff moms feel for their children on days when both mothers and kids are unusually well-behaved. I was mesmerized by how Daniel would reach across the seat and hold Benjamin's hand, as Ben eyed him from his car seat. As brothers, these two would get to experience growing up together. When people asked how he felt about having a baby brother, Daniel would respond with one of his wide smiles and say, "We're going to trash the place."

"You two are adorable," I said, giving them my full attention. Then I saw it. There was something on the left side of Daniel's neck, right there under the jawbone. Maybe it was the way the sun was shining on it. Perhaps it was a bruise I hadn't noticed before. Daniel was the adventurous type, and sometimes that energy resulted in injured knees and elbows. As I got the boys out of their car seats, I looked closer at Daniel's neck. It looked like a bump was seated underneath the skin on a gland.

Daniel was eager to get out of the van. "Get Benny out, too, Mommy. Let's go!"

"Just a minute. Hold on. Turn your head to the right."

Daniel turned to the left, the right, and back to the left like a bobblehead. That caused Ben to laugh, so Daniel repeated the action, and then I had two laughing boys. I unbuckled their seatbelts, and Daniel stood by me as I lifted Ben into the umbrella stroller. The air was full of spring's scents. In two months, we were headed to Japan for a family vacation to see my parents. There was much to be thankful for. I pushed worry aside.

After we ate, I wiped syrup off Daniel's cheeks, and he rushed to the playground. Baby Ben sat in his stroller by the table where he and I watched Daniel play. Daniel jumped into the colorful plastic ball pit and then climbed out of them to sail down the small slide back into them.

What was that on his neck?

A feeling of dread came over me, starting in my gut and moving upward.

It's nothing, it's nothing. Of course, it's nothing.

When we got home, I decided asking my neighbor for her opinion wouldn't be too much of a bother. Debbie, a nurse at both UNC-Hospitals and Duke Medical Center, came to our house to take a look at Daniel's neck.

Getting Daniel to stand still while she scanned his face and neck took some coaxing. After Debbie removed her fingers from the lump, I nodded that he could return to the family room to finish building a tower with Legos.

Debbie said, "I'd schedule an appointment."

"What do you think it is?" I looked into her eyes to determine how serious she thought this was.

"Just call your pediatrician and have her take a look at it."

They squeezed us into an appointment with the pediatrician the next day. Dr. Lancaster didn't know what the lump was, but she had a few colleagues examine Daniel.

"Could be Cat Scratch Fever," said one of the middle-aged doctors. He wore a white lab coat, his name embroidered over his heart. His black-rimmed glasses made him look professional and intelligent. Even so, I almost busted out in laughter. Was Cat Scratch Fever an actual ailment? Or was this doctor trying to be funny without cracking a smile?

I had to ask. "What is Cat Scratch Fever?"

"Do you have a cat?" the doctor asked.

"No."

"My daddy's allergic to cats," Daniel told the group. He felt that answered why we did not own a cat.

Dr. Lancaster smiled. "We'll send his blood work to the Centers for Disease Control to see what they think it is." She prescribed amoxicillin for ten days.

~*~
Five

Once we had acknowledged and addressed the lump, it seemed to have permission to make itself known by swelling. Within a few days, it stuck out of Daniel's neck like a goutier.

"Does it hurt?" I asked Daniel.

"No," he said, as he played in the family room with his Matchbox trucks.

The doctors had asked the same thing, and Daniel had said it did not hurt. It looked like it should be painful.

I took Daniel in to see Dr. Lancaster again, telling her the gland was not shrinking, even though Daniel had been on antibiotics for six days. I didn't need to make a fuss; anyone could see that the lump had grown and was not going away.

Surgery was suggested, and, when we met with Dr. Blair, a surgeon recommended by Dr. Lancaster, he was confident he could drain the area.

The morning of surgery, Daniel was hungry and wanted to eat breakfast, but we'd been instructed he was to have no food before the procedure.

"You can eat later," I said, as David drove our van across town to Durham Regional Hospital.

"Can I have pancakes?" Daniel asked from his car seat. "And Mountain Doom."

Not a fan of Mountain Dew myself, the name Doom seemed appropriate. I never corrected him when he called the soft drink this. Rachel had coined it, by mistake, of course. And we let her call it that because parents do that. The cute "isms" of our children are what we remember and look forward to retelling, especially when they become teens and wish we'd stop with the embarrassing remembrances.

We distracted Daniel, so by the time we arrived at the hospital, he was occupied with other things, like our family lists of firsts: "Rachel learned to talk first, I learned to walk first, and Benny got fat first." He giggled and repeated the list, as David pulled into a parking space. I was grateful Baby Ben was not with us that morning, so my attention could be solely on Daniel. Susan had offered to take care of him.

When it was time for Daniel's surgery, we hugged and kissed him, our hearts vulnerable. Then we watched our son take the hand of the young, tall anesthesiologist. The two—patient and professional—walked down the hall toward the operating room. I sat glued to the scene until I couldn't see either of their backs anymore. After that, I tried to read to take my mind off of my son going under the knife. I opened the newest Dean Koontz novel. David had brought another one of Koontz's books to read. We were both fans of this author's strange and enticing stories.

Hours later, Dr. Blair entered the waiting room. He planted himself on the back of a lone sofa. I got up and walked closer to him. David put his book aside, ready to listen.

"You're going to be disappointed," the doctor said.

What was this gibberish? Disappointed about what?

"I wasn't able to drain as much of the area as I had hoped. It's not liquid, but more like a cottage cheese type of material."

As I tried to imagine what cottage cheese looks like inside a person's neck, Dr. Blair said, "Don't worry. It's not cancer. I'll check for TB."

After dinner that night, the five of us went outside to sit under the starry sky. Daniel had a large white bandage on his neck where the growth had been lanced. Feeling playful, he stood by the street light and threw his plastic blue medical wristband into the air. When it landed on our lawn, he grabbed the band and tossed it up again. Our friends, Doug, Emily, and their four-year-old daughter, Sophie, came to check on us. Daniel wanted Sophie to play this toss-and-retrieve game. He showed her how it was done. The wristband went up, and then Daniel searched for it once it landed. Our lawn needed a lawnmower's trim; the blades were high, so the searching took time.

Sophie stood by Daniel but was not interested in the game.

"He seems in good spirits," said Emily.

The next morning, the Friday of Memorial Day weekend, Ben and Daniel napped, while I sat on the sofa reading Dean Koontz and ignoring the sighs from the dust bunnies in the living room. This was Mom Time, and I chose not to spend it cleaning, cooking, or paying bills.

When the phone rang, I let the answering machine kick on until I heard the voice of our pediatrician, and only then did I pick up, carrying the cordless phone from the nearby kitchen to the sofa. Dr. Lancaster got right to the point. There were no pleasantries or inquiries about our holiday weekend plans.

"Malignant," I think I heard her say. "It's a small-round-blue-cell tumor."

Seated on the sofa, clutching the phone, I stared at the blue valances along our family room windows. They were dotted in small circles, round like cells.

I wanted to believe Dr. Lancaster was delirious or "off her rocker," an expression I'd grown up hearing from my mother. I waited for her to pause, so I could tell her she'd made a mistake. In about an hour, Daniel would wake from sleeping, come downstairs, and ask for a cup of apple juice because that was his favorite. Benjamin would wake, I'd nurse him, and Daniel would venture outside to check on the tomato vines in the garden, wanting to pick green ones even though I'd told him we don't pick green tomatoes. Rachel would get off the school bus, eager to tell me about her day.

"You need to pick up lab results from Durham Regional and take them to UNC," said Dr. Lancaster.

My mind tracked back to reality. "UNC? Don't people with cancer go to Duke?" Everyone in Durham knows Duke Medical Center is famous for its oncology care.

"Your insurance covers UNC. You'll like the hospital; it's more personable than Duke."

I wondered if she was allowed to admit that; she was employed by Duke.

"I'm sorry to be the bearer of bad news."

The conversation ended; I sat still on the sofa with a pen and paper I didn't recall picking up. But I'd taken notes. *Durham Regional. UNC. Lab results. Small round blue cell tumor.* My limbs were stuck; my mind felt suspended somewhere over the room. Although I knew I needed to do something, I needed to figure out where to begin.

The day before, Daniel had a lance-able swell in his neck. Today, my son had cancer.

I pressed the speed dial on the cordless phone for David's office.

I don't remember what I said, but it got him home in record time.

~*~
Six

Saturday mornings were relaxed, with late breakfasts and lots of coffee for David and me. Ben and Rachel shared the recliner to watch cartoons. When Elizabeth could sit without the help of her high chair, she'd crawl to the middle of the family room and plant herself upright. Sometimes she showed interest in the shows her siblings liked. On other mornings she cared more about playing with her dolls and blocks. I always pictured a healthy Daniel with the three. He wasn't bald; he had his before-chemo blond hair. Where would he sit? What would he want to watch? How would he interact with Liz?

On a Saturday at the end of November, the first November since Daniel's death, Liz banged on a plastic toy drum that had belonged to Daniel. Over the noise, David suggested we go to the cemetery.

"You mean all of us?" I asked and poured another mug of French Roast.

"Yeah."

"Now?"

He had designated every Thursday night as his night to go there. After helping to put the kids to bed, he'd take off. He sat in the dark at Daniel's grave with a can of beer and a cigar. In between sips and puffs, he'd talk to Daniel. He was so well known at the cemetery, that when one of the grounds crew would spot him, he'd ask, "Are you here to see Daniel?"

The ritual still felt far from normal to me. My thoughts were congested with things like, *When I get there, I'll have to face the small grave and all my usual wondering of why we even visit cemeteries. Why do we take flowers, fresh or artificial?* Going to Markham Memorial Gardens for Daniel's birthday seemed like a bereaved parent sort of thing to do because friends in my support group did that on their child's birth dates. But going as a family on a regular day, on an ordinary morning, made me wonder what we would do there.

"We can pick up food on the way and eat it there," said David, as though reading my mind.

I thought of my grandmother Hall, fondly known as Patsie, who'd take flowers to place on tombstones at the family cemetery in Amelia County Courthouse, Virginia. I went with her once when I was eighteen, and we visited the dairy and tobacco country of my ancestry. I thought: You know, these people under the tombs are not here and are too busy enjoying heaven to even notice you have spent

$24.99 on a bouquet of roses with sprigs of baby's breath.

Why not take some flowers? My inner voice and often critic asked. I've named her Breezy because of the way she breezes in and out of my thoughts. *Take some flowers. It can help with that guilt you have.*

After I'd had one of those days when I thought my mind was being bashed apart, David had brought home a bouquet for me. They sat in a clear vase on the kitchen table. Now I wouldn't have to worry about buying flowers. As David told the kids to prepare for our outing, I clipped some daisies and carnations and wrapped the bottoms of their stems in a wet paper towel to keep them from drying out.

We piled into the van with our children and diaper bags. Once there, we sat on a blanket under the oak by Daniel's grave and ate biscuits and hash browns we'd picked up at the Hardee's' drive-through. Elizabeth sat in her car seat carrier, watching the overhead tree branches. David placed a hash brown on Daniel's grave above his engraved name. The ants found it and were delighted.

When we finished our meal, David took Rachel and Ben across the field to the American flag fluttering in the autumn breeze. Minutes after they left, Elizabeth opened her lungs and let out a fierce cry. I removed her from her car seat carrier and sat in the back of the van to nurse her. I stroked her delicate skin and watched her eyelids close like a butterfly's wings. "Daniel, I wish you were here to make some cute comments about your new sister," I said.

He had been excited when Ben arrived, marveling at the infant's "*wuddle* hands and *wuddle* feet." During treatments, Daniel chatted with the nurses in the hospital about the baby growing in my womb. "It's the size of a raisin," he told them. When they laughed, I thought, *That was my line; I was the one who'd told him about the size of a raisin.* But using my word was a form of flattery; he had found the raisin reference funny, as had I.

"Do you want the baby to be a boy or a girl?" his favorite nurse asked when checking his blood pressure.

"I hope it's a girl baby. We already have a boy baby."

Elizabeth woke, and I carried her from the van to view the epitaphs on the graves by Daniel's. There were tributes to loving wives and husbands, sisters, and brothers. Being in a place filled with death, I thought of my own. Although the hope I would die had faded, ever since Daniel's death, I knew it was no longer something that only happened to the very old. Continuing my trek among the graves, I wondered what my epitaph would say when I was gone and buried. Perhaps: *No flowers needed; she doesn't believe in wasting money.*

~*~

My Dear Daniel,

Today was a special day of remembering you. We went to visit your grave. Although I forgot the camera, I hope to remember the beauty of the day. The sky was clear, and a light wind blew the oak leaves. We picked up Hardee's biscuits and ate breakfast on a picnic blanket on the grass by your marker. I put some yellow daisies and white carnations in a flower pot near your grave. (The flowers were from a large bouquet given to me by Daddy when I was having a bad day because you are gone. The flower pot is from Susan; she planted tomato vines, knowing how much you loved tomatoes.) Rachel brought your blue plastic chair and her gray one for her and Benjamin to sit in. She added stickers to your marker. Elizabeth grew fussy and cried and later took a short nap under the oak by your grave. I smelled what I thought was doggie poop, but it was Ben. Daddy changed his diaper. I walked among the graves, carrying Elizabeth with me. Then when we were ready to go home, my shirt was covered in baby poop. Elizabeth's diaper had leaked through and onto me. Daddy again changed a nasty diaper, putting Elizabeth into one of Benny's diapers, because your sister's diaper bag was empty.

We miss you so much. We think of you all the time. We've met other moms and dads who have also had a child die. Tonight, we had one of them over for dinner. Her name is Caralie, and she lost her son Bryan forty years ago to the same cancer you had. Her story is in a book we were given, and, when I found out she lives nearby in Raleigh, I called and was invited to her home for lunch. You've probably met her son Bryan in Heaven. While y'all are up there, we're down here talking about how our lives have changed since you left us.

How we wish you were still here with us. How lonely we feel without your radiance, without your beautiful smile.
Mommy

Putting words onto paper as I thought of Daniel made me feel close to him. I loved the life-giving feeling writing gave me. I had spent so much time reviewing all the details of his death, chastising myself for not knowing a staph infection had been brewing in his body on that January morning. I had no lack in the guilt department. But when I wrote to him, it was as though I could shine the light on his life and not dwell on his death.

Caralie was a gift that came to me after reading a book of accounts by local bereaved moms and dads. One of David's co-workers gave the book to him days after Daniel died. Since Caralie's son had neuroblastoma, I searched in the phone book for her number. When I called her, she invited me to lunch at her home in Raleigh. I got lost; it was before GPS systems, and I was late. But she had kept the tuna casserole warm in the oven. As we ate and talked, I knew the sadness of losing a child lingers even after forty years. Caralie cried as she recalled her son's favorite restaurant.

So much for those who insisted *I would get over this*. Many wanted me to laugh and not be sad, to know Daniel was *in a better place*, and to move on, get on with life. People like happiness; they don't want to mess with tears, tissues, and torn hearts.

~*~
Seven

What do I do with God?

The fantasy of escaping my situation wasn't an option. No disappearing acts. No running from the day-to-day sorrow. I had to bumble through. Disappointed, and angry with God, I needed to protect myself from expecting anything from him ever again. If God and I were at a party together, God was someone to just nod at across the table. I didn't want to need to converse, to pray, and I certainly didn't want to ever have to ask him or his son for anything, certainly not for the life of a loved one. I didn't want to depend on God, Jesus, or the Holy Spirit because that meant having to trust the Trinity. I had trusted God, and I let him know that. "I trusted Daniel to you," I reminded God. "I expected you to make him well. Instead, you let him die."

Talking honestly with other Christians who would listen about my frustration over God allowing Daniel's death was helpful. Caralie wanted me to know God didn't take our suffering from us; he gave himself to us. I revisited the Psalms and was grateful for the verses that spoke of wondering where God is in seasons of distraught.

But one day, all my grief work, all the ground I had covered with not being mad at God, with trying to heal, with getting some hope back into my life, dissolved.

Dr. Art wanted us to come to his office to tell us about Daniel's autopsy results. David and I were confident the treatments had not removed the cancer cells from our child's body. We figured the tumor had been too aggressive. But we were in for a shock!

"No cancer cells were found," Dr. Art told us as we sat across from him.

"What do you mean?" I had a newborn again, and thanks to her, I wasn't getting much sleep. Perhaps I hadn't heard the oncologist correctly.

"The autopsy showed no cancer."

David and I sat confused, our minds spinning.

"However," Dr. Art quickly added, "that doesn't mean that the cancer would not have come back. But from what we can see, there were no cancer cells anywhere."

No cancer, no cancer, no cancer. The two words banged in my head. I blurted, "He would have lived just as long, or maybe even longer, if we hadn't made him go through chemo."

Calmly, Dr. Art responded. "I would have called child protective services if you hadn't allowed Daniel to be treated."

I supposed that was the oncologist's way of reassuring us that we'd had no choice but to put Daniel through the eight months of chemo, surgeries, and radiation. We had done what we had to do.

But I was not easily reassured. Rage filled me, and on the drive home to Durham, I hollered. David was equally distraught.

"The treatment killed our child while killing the cancer," he said. "They wanted the autopsy done." He was referring to Daniel's oncology team. "Now they can say their treatments worked."

"It's a slap in the face. All that Daniel had to endure, and then, after he's dead we get to find out for the first time that he's cancer-free. It doesn't matter now."

Our son was gone.

What a stupid autopsy.

The memory of Daniel going to the hospital chapel to pray for God to heal his *boo-boo*, even kneeling beside a chair, his infusion pole by his side, was a memory that made me reach for more tissues. If a little boy asks God to heal him in a chapel, how can there be any reply from God but, "Of course"?

Missionaries in Japan, churches in Durham and beyond, had prayed for his cancer to leave, and it had. "Why?!" I shouted toward Heaven one starry night. "You do know that we wanted him cancer-free and living, right?" I'm sure that cancer-free and dead wasn't part of anyone's prayers.

I had a long list of things we had prayed for, but had not received, including the first planned trip to visit my parents we had to cancel when Daniel was diagnosed. The latter Make-a-Wish trip seemed hopeful, but the day before we were to leave, Daniel had a fever and ended up in the hospital for a week. We had our Thanksgiving meal at the hospital, thanks to its food services, and were glad to see Daniel eat turkey, green beans, sweet potatoes, and dressing. He seldom had an appetite. Our glee was short-lived; an hour later, he threw up.

When he was unexpectedly admitted to the hospital again, we spent Christmas on the pediatric oncology ward. As I slept next to Daniel in a chair that made into an uncomfortable bed, my thoughts were: *Next Christmas Daniel will be back to health and we'll have a great family Christmas at home.*

~*~

As we approached that dreaded *next Christmas*, our first Christmas without Daniel, we went as a family to the cemetery to decorate Daniel's grave. We stuck a giant candy cane lawn ornament into the dirt by his marker. We laid a Christmas wreath on top of his grave. While there, I searched and found Melanie's son's grave. Melanie was a new friend from a church we'd started to attend. When she heard about Daniel, she told me that her thirteen-month-old son was also buried at Markham Memorial Gardens. Colin's marker had an inscription that promised: *We will hold you in our hearts.*

"Oh, Colin," I said, as I hovered over his resting place. "Too young, too little." I knew how Colin had died. He took his last breath right behind his father, and then he drowned. His father had been fixated on looking for his wedding ring that had fallen into the pool. Preoccupied, he hadn't seen or heard his son pull himself up onto the arm of a deck chair and walk it and himself over the pool's edge into the water. While the tragedy was horrific, Melanie and her husband had worked through their turmoil together. Seeing my angst one evening, Melanie had invited me to forgive myself. She was a nurse, and after hearing my detailed medical account of Daniel's last days, reassured me there was nothing I could have done to save my son.

But, at the grave, I still had questions. I touched her son's marker. "How have they dealt with that harrowing ending?" I asked. "How have they forgiven and carried on?"

A breeze blew over Colin's marker, rattling fallen oak leaves.

"How will I?"

There were no easy answers. There was only this day, this one-day-at-a-time existence.

All the books on parental grief said you had to walk through grief, and the journey has no shortcuts. They also emphasized grief is the price of love. If I didn't love Daniel, there would be no reason to have to adjust and adapt to a life without him each and every day. When I sought after books written by Christians—those who knew the suffering that accompanies loss—I looked for any doubts they might have for God. By the time most of the authors wrote their stories, they had forgotten complicated issues they'd had with their faith, or they had chosen not to write about their doubts. I looked for honesty. I wanted authentic accounts.

Sometimes, I concluded not everyone was like me; not everyone was bombarded with the need to sort through a messy faith.

~*~
Eight

In the summer, we brought watermelon to the cemetery because of what it symbolized for us. It's beautiful how objects and food hold memories after a loved one leaves. We hold onto these and make more over them because it is all we have left. Friends talked about recipes they enjoyed that their grandmas had served. Others wore jewelry, a ring, or a necklace, that had belonged to a mother who had gone too soon. Memories replace the living and breathing person we once held and spoke with, and, while we need them, they are a poor substitute for a loved one. Daniel was vibrant, funny, adorable, and creative, and now he was reduced to memories.

As I tried to focus on happy moments instead of Daniel's last days when he was wheeled to the ER after a routine oncology clinic visit, the memories that threaded through my heart were of the many watermelon stories. When he was diagnosed, my parents flew into Durham from Japan, where they served as career missionaries and where I was born. Mom bought a watermelon at a grocery store outing, and we ate it outside after dinner on a June evening. The adults used spoons and forks, but Daniel sat on the driveway, placed his slice in front of him, and lunged into it. I snapped a photo. A bandage was on one side of his neck where he'd just had surgery. But the amusing part was that Daniel dug in face first while his sister Rachel sat next to him gingerly eating her slice. Watermelons connected with Daniel. The first example of his love of watermelon began in the grocery store. The final one ended in the bathtub.

Our family was—and still is—enthusiastic about fireworks. There was a time David even slipped in some illegal in North Carolina, the kind purchased across the border in his state of South Carolina. Every Fourth of July, we sat on our lawn in anticipation. David stood yards in front of us on the street and lit the torpedo buzz, the rockets, all the funny-sounding popping crackers. We cheered and clapped and buried our faces in ripe slices of watermelon.

July 4, 1996, Daniel was in the hospital having his monthly chemo injections. Our celebration of our nation's birthday would have to be held inside Daniel's hospital room. Daniel looked forward to watching the fireworks, hoping his hospital room window would provide a good view. But a nurse informed us there wouldn't be fireworks from Kenan Stadium that night; the reason was unclear.

Daniel bounced back from his disappointment when friends Sue, and her twelve-year-old daughter, Becca, entered the room with a watermelon and a knife. "We came to celebrate July Fourth with you!" said Sue in her vibrant Rochester, New York, accent.

Sue cut slices for each of us and served them on paper plates. Becca placed a plate on Daniel's tray table.

Daniel dipped his mouth into the fruit. With juice running down his cheeks and chin, he took another bite. He found a black seed and, facing Becca, spat the seed toward her and then, grinning, waited for her reaction.

She laughed; he filled his lungs and cheeks with air and let out another. It landed on his sheet. Our family comes from a long line of watermelon-seed-spitters. Mom had won contests, but it looked like Daniel needed some tips from her.

After the two left, Daniel said, "I think I've had enough watermelon." He lay on the bed, comically rubbing his tummy and grinning.

I looked at the half-consumed treat. It was too big to store in the fridge in the communal kitchen down the corridor. "Where can we put it?" Where did other patients keep their watermelons?

I'd read the thick binder about Daniel's medications and various procedures, but nowhere in any of the literature was there a section about proper protocol for taking care of leftover fruit.

"How about in the bathtub?" Daniel said.

What a great idea! "Why not?"

And so, we did just that.

~*~

Before I noticed the lump on his neck, before surgery, before the pediatrician called on the Friday of Memorial Day weekend to say it was cancer—"a small-blue-round-cell tumor named neuroblastoma"—before chemo, and additional surgeries, we had a different life.

Daniel and I went shopping at the local grocery store.

"Can we get a watermelon?" Daniel asked as I wheeled the shopping cart—or what southerners call *buggy*—through the produce section. He rode on the back of the cart, one leg dangling while the other balanced his weight.

I glanced at the watermelons. They were oblong, a shape I still need to get used to—watermelons are round in Japan. Regardless of form, these watermelons in a cardboard box before us with the price tag of $7.99 couldn't be real. They had to be greenhouse-grown. It was the end of March. "We'll get one when it's watermelon season." I hoped that promise would assuage his interest.

"When is watermelon season?"

"July. Summer. When it gets hot." I picked up a bag of potatoes for a scalloped potato dish and a bunch of bananas ripe enough for banana bread. I wheeled the buggy away from the green-house grown objects. I looked forward to a ripe, red watermelon, the kind where juice runs down your chin and fingers, the kind that is sweet and makes you remember childhood.

Daniel was three. He'd have plenty of time to enjoy watermelons ripened under the summer sun and spit those slippery black seeds across the lawn.

~*~

It's Always Watermelon Season became our family mantra. Don't put things off. Go on the trip. Don't wait till tomorrow; don't expect to be healthy and able to do what you want to do then. Live today. Today is all we have. Get the greenhouse-grown watermelon.

I wrote an article about watermelon memories and how our family held a new outlook on life. I sent the piece to a bereavement publication. When it was published, I gave copies to friends. From there, the gifts—tokens of remembrance—arrived in my mailbox. I hadn't expected any of this. Friends sent stickers, stationary, and a wind chime—all with watermelons on them. A friend from college sent a rug in the shape of a slice of watermelon, a beach towel, and plastic bowls. Friends in Japan sent a mobile, earrings, and a fan, all with the round red delicacy on a green rind sprinkled with black seeds.

~*~

Nine

David was instrumental in planning outings for our
family and then helping to get the kids ready to go
to the park, to the mall, or to the cemetery. One
afternoon, our family outing was to a cemetery in
the nearby town of Hillsborough—the Old Town
Cemetery by the Presbyterian Church. The city has
deemed this place, constructed in 1757, a historical
site. I'm sure one of the reasons is because the body
of William Hooper, one of the signers of the
Declaration of Independence, is famously buried
there. Much later, I learned he has two burial sites.
Over one hundred years after William's death and
burial in Hillsborough, North Carolina, the Guilford
Battleground Company had the idea to gather the
bodies of the three North Carolina signers of the
Declaration and erect a memorial. So, William
Hooper, Joseph Hewes, and John Penn were re-
interred on the site of the 1781 Battle at Guilford
Courthouse. None of these men fought in the battle,

as explained at the memorial created for them known as the Signers Monument. But the rumor is not all of William's remains were transported to the monument. It is believed that part of him still rests under his tomb in Hillsborough.

As David, the kids, and I meandered among the tombstones, the engraving on the creamy white tomb of a young woman got my attention. I copied the words from the epitaph into a notebook, because nothing on any of the tombstones compared with these thoughtful words on the grave of Mary Shaw:

Sacred to the memory of Mary Shaw
24 years
March 9th, 1840
She needs no formal record of her virtues on this cold marble. They are deeply graven on the tablets of many warm and loving hearts, in which her memory is tenderly and sacredly cherished.

I wondered what kind of friend, parent, or spouse this Mary had been. Whoever decided on these words was undoubtedly a creative soul.

~*~

In New Bern, one of my favorite coastal towns, David, the kids, and I took a trolley tour of the city. One of the stops was the cemetery. The stories of the Union and Confederate soldiers told by our guide were fascinating. But the words on the tombstones of children held my focus. They used to write on the infant graves the exact age of the child who'd died–*"Jeremy Hawthorne, infant son of Zachary and Millie Hawthorne, nine months, two weeks and three days old."* Some parents in my bereavement group knew the exact age of their deceased child. They had it down to how many years, months, days, and hours their child had lived. I've never been good at math, so I stuck with just shy of four and a half years.

The only scary thing about a cemetery is the fear of what others will say about us and place on our stones when we are six feet under. Will I be remembered lovingly? Will anyone miss me? Will friends and family cherish who I was to them? What legacy will I leave behind? Once I'm in heaven, will what my legacy is or people's thoughts of me matter?

A sobering revelation hits me each time I wander among the dead—my life on earth is but a speck on the timeline of history. Yet, hallelujah, this brief life is not all I get! My soul will live forever.

~*~

Many Fridays, we'd meet David at Daniel's Place. On his way to the cemetery from work, he'd pick up pizzas or burgers for our dinner. Once together, we'd spread towels on the grass and eat. On a summer evening, when the kids grew tired of tossing the Frisbee and wanted to walk up the gravel road with David to the mausoleum, I stayed behind. I strolled among the grave markers. There was one behind Daniel's marker on the other side of the oak I had not seen before. The words on the top right corner are: *We're so glad you came*. Under his name, it reads *Our Son*. Taylor has only one day etched on his stone, March 19, 2000.

I knew nothing about this boy or his parents or how he died. But the brevity of his life made me weak in my knees. I stopped at the grave as my mind questioned. Did Taylor get to take a breath? Was his death a surprise, or did his mama know he was not destined to live long? Was he stillborn? How did Taylor's parents remember him? Did they keep the blanket he was wrapped in on the one day he lived? Did they get prints of his hands and feet? Did they have other children? Did they feel cheated they never heard his voice, saw him walk, eat Cheerios in his high chair, or face plant into a slice of watermelon? Kneeling on the grass, I ran a finger over Taylor's name. What memories did they cherish, and why did they get so few? Had his mama run a finger across his cheek, over his earlobe, and prayed that God would spare him, give him endless breaths, let him grow old?

It was hard to imagine how parents made sense of life when their babies were born to die. Did Taylor's parents look at the night sky and ask, "What was the purpose?"

~*~
Ten

Before we named it Daniel's Place, the cemetery
was a grassy region with Daniel's name engraved on
a stone much too small for a boy who had called
himself a Brave Cookie. It was a sea of graves
without a single Daniel memory. The garden, by the
side of the house where Daniel and I had grown
tomatoes, and our home, held Daniel's memories. I
often went to IBM Park to write by the weeping
willows on the pond's edge. I felt connected to
Daniel there, since that was where he'd played in
the sandbox and on the swings. It was where my
heart sank into my stomach that day he'd decided to
climb the highest slide. He was only a little over a
year old. Rachel had only attempted it a few days
before he had, and she was two years older. The
park was where Daniel and I had listened to the
train whistle as an Amtrak made its way toward
Raleigh.

While David continued to go to the grave each Thursday, I was unsure how the location would become part of our lives. It took a family outing to help me understand how a place of remembrance can make a family seem like no one is missing.

~*~

The five of us were out at a restaurant, having just finished burgers, when Liz crawled under the table to retrieve her napkin. A woman walked by our table on the way to pay her bill.

"You have two kids?" she asked and smiled at Ben and Rachel, who were sipping the last mouthfuls of juice. Before I could reply, the stranger said, "I have three."

Right then, Liz popped up from under the table, napkin in hand.

"Oh," said the woman, letting out a laugh that showed amusement. "You have three."

"I have four," I said.

"One is missing?"

"Yes," I said, hoping I didn't sound hesitant. "One is missing."

At the cemetery, no one was missing. When the maintenance crew saw David and me with three children racing, laughing, and doing handstands, they knew we were there to see Daniel. They knew we had four kids.

~*~

As Daniel's Place became part of us, we grew protective. One Saturday, we saw changes had occurred. Trees to the west of the cemetery had been cleared. Months later, construction started; new homes were built. We were sorry to see the complete woods that had surrounded the grounds had houses, houses visible from Daniel's grave.

"I hope they don't take down trees and build a subdivision in the other woods," I said. "We need those woods to stay intact." *Those woods* were to the north and where David had taken Rachel to pee when she was desperate. One day, my modesty might wane, and I'd be brave enough to pee there.

~*~

When local grocery stores decided, for whatever reason, to sell the oblong spheres without seeds, I muttered, "Why? What is the point of not having seeds to spit?" They were proud of this new variety, posting signs in the windows: *Seedless watermelons!* I searched for ones with black seeds, not because I wanted to spray them across the yard, but because these sticky seeds were part of who Daniel had been.

We were at the neighborhood pool on a summer afternoon, drying off from a swim, when Liz, who had turned four, reminded me, "Daniel didn't only like watermelon."

"Oh, really?" Amused to hear what a sibling who had never met her brother had to tell me, I waited for more.

"Yes," she said, without any hesitation. "He liked Thomas the Tank Engine."

"That's right, he did." I stretched my gifted watermelon towel over a pool chair. Liz had a relationship with Daniel that baffled me. What must it be like to grow up with a brother that you only had the shared memories of others to rely on? As she grew older, would she feel cheated that she had never seen his smile or heard his voice?

These kinds of thoughts were always present. Years before, I realized that growing up with the cemetery had a downside.

I'd picked Ben from preschool, and we were on our way home.

From the back seat, I heard, "I wanna go playground. I wanna go playground!"

We were at a traffic light, and none of the places where he'd played—McDonald's golden arches, park, or playground with slides—were in sight. "We need to get home," I said. "No playground now, okay?"

Using the rearview mirror, I glanced at my two-year-old and saw he was fixated on a plot of land with tombstones adorned with flowers. And that's when I realized Ben thought cemeteries were playgrounds. I wanted to laugh, but I was also tempted to cry.

~*~

We worry. That's because we're parents. Bereaved parents agonize in other ways, like how our surviving children and the ones who come after the child who died will cope. There are days when thinking about how to best handle parenting exhausts us. I hadn't always been uncertain or confused; there was a time when I'd been a confident mother, strong in my beliefs I would provide a safe and loving home for my kids. I'd had no fears in the motherhood department.

After Daniel's death, we'd taken Rachel to a therapist because it was recommended by the hospital staff. As Rachel entered an office with the professional and the door shut, I wondered what the verdict would be. Would the therapist find that my daughter showed abnormal behavior because of the loss of her best friend, her brother? What was Rachel telling her? If Rachel needed continual therapy sessions, could we afford them?

When the session ended and the two emerged from the meeting room, the therapist approached me. "She's fine," she said, which made me want to dance. "She's going to be just fine."

But David was not fine. For a decade after Daniel's death, I used the tools of writing and speaking about the value of writing through grief and loss to survive. David's tools for survival were medications and alcohol.

~*~
Eleven

David isolated himself in the bathroom where he read books on near-death experiences and drank from jugs of cheap red wine and cans of beer. Sometimes, I'd find him seated on the floor with his head against the edge of the bathtub. I'd try to wake him, but his slumber was deep. "I fell asleep," he'd tell me the next morning when I asked him about it. The children overheard us, and after that, he and the kids would joke about Daddy falling asleep in the bathtub.

Years before, I'd encouraged David to write, and he wrote a short memory about the Saturday ritual of when he, Rachel, and Daniel ate breakfasts at McDonald's. He also wrote a poem about his disappointment with God.

And then, in 2004, he started to write again. He had a list for me, composed in his perfect handwriting.

1) Have a light snack after kids go to bed
2) Drink only 1 beer
3) Do a word search puzzle
4) Read from 9 till 10 PM
5) Play a game with Alice from 10 PM till bedtime

I gathered this list was some way for me to hold him accountable to following his timeline. I'd be ready at 10 p.m. to play *You Don't Know Jack* on the computer, or a board game, or Boggle. It was unusual whenever I beat him at Boggle, but, when I did, I cheered.

Weeks after the first list, a two-page email popped into my inbox. The form was similar, but the list had more detail. He wanted me to make him even more accountable, down to how many pages he read in his sci-fi book and, once again, he emphasized *only one beer*.

Days passed; there was another message. David claimed that I was enabling him. Enabling? I had to look the word up in the dictionary.

I asked him about the messages and the lists, and he gave me a book to read about a marriage in danger. There were statements and questions to fill in, and it felt like I was back in school, or having a dream where I was presented with a test and I had no idea how to pass it because I hadn't studied.

He said we needed to separate.

"Why?" I asked. "Why would we need to do that?"

"I think we need to live apart for the next six months."

We had moved to another neighborhood in

Durham that was zoned for better schools. The mortgage was more than our other home had been, and I couldn't see how we could afford two households.

"I'm going to move to an Extended Stay motel," David said. "Don't worry about money. I'll use the money in my 401K."

When had living with him become like living with a stranger? Even though it had not been easy dealing with his distant ways, I didn't want him to move out. Separation was for other couples, but not us! He said we could read the book he'd given me and go to marriage counseling together. I tried the book; we tried therapy. The marriage counselor scolded Amanda, David's current therapist he saw each week, accusing her of being more of a friend and confidant than helping him with his issues. The only question she asked me was if I wanted to stay in the marriage; I said I did. Then she turned to David to berate his therapist.

David moved into an Extended Stay motel and invited the kids to visit him on weekends. I couldn't keep my child alive; I couldn't keep my husband from living apart from me. I dove into my writing and pushed my head further into the sand. Together with my muse, I worked, and soon I'd be in my happy place. I kept article ideas in my notebooks, on slips of paper, receipts, splashed along the phone bill. I filled *Tributes*, my ezine I had created and sent out once a month, with resources to help the brokenhearted. I included tips on how to write from pain. Sometimes I heard from subscribers who'd tell me how much my article on honoring a dead child's memory helped them on their grief journey.

~*~

Surely we could make our marriage work. There had to be a way. Three months into the separation, I asked David to come back to our house to live. He was reluctant at first, but, after we agreed on what changes we needed to work on, he moved out of the motel. Having him back home made the kids happy. Shortly after he was living with us again, he lost his software job. He looked for another. When he was invited for an interview, I hugged him. He got the job at Lenovo but was bummed because it was only a temporary one to last a year. I was grateful he was once again employed.

One night when the kids were asleep, and I was writing in the living room, David entered the room and showed me a note he'd scrawled. In messy print that didn't look like his handwriting I'd always admired, it read: *Please go away. I am fine. I don't need to go to the hospital. GO AWAY!*

I looked up from the note. "What is this about?"

"I took medication," he said. "I took . . . a lot." His words were slurred, his eyes hazy, like he was unable to focus. "Dr. Preston said she had to call to send an ambulance for me."

"An ambulance is coming here?"

He opened the front door. I watched him tape his note by the doorbell.

"Will they see that?" It all felt odd to me, but much of his recent behavior had been strange—the lists, the emails accusing me of not caring about our relationship, the drinking, the weight gain, and then the rapid weight loss.

"I don't need to go to the hospital," he said.

As I sat beside him on the sofa, I probed, trying to understand. He had a list he read to his therapist over the phone of all the meds he took.

"Are they really coming for you?" I asked.

Days earlier, he was convinced someone had stolen a letter he wrote out of our mailbox. He said that he had an idea for a revolutionary product, and he was going to get a patent for it, but someone followed him on the way home, and, the next day, the letter was gone. He was convinced a person had followed him home and taken his letter from the mailbox.

Over the next half hour, David shifted in and out of sleep while I shifted from pity to annoyance and aggravation. I'd been annoyed about David's lengthy letters to me and my inability to know how to help him. I'd wished him back to his old self where he'd taken loving interest in our lives. These days, I was the only one driving kids to school, helping with homework, cooking, and cleaning, while he zoned out.

By eleven-thirty, I felt myself drifting to sleep. I forced myself awake. "I don't think anyone is coming," I said.

David was asleep; his head of thick, wavy hair was planted against the back of the sofa. Minutes passed, he briefly opened his eyes, and then mumbled something.

"I'm going to bed." I wasn't sure David had heard me. I headed upstairs. Lying in bed, I listened for the sound of tires, the doorbell, voices. I doubted there was an overdose or ambulance. David was conjuring up fabrications in his head.

In the morning, his car was in the driveway, but he was not on the sofa, where he often spent the night. I couldn't find him. He was gone.

Later in the day, after we'd returned from church, the phone rang. David had been taken to the hospital and wanted to see the kids. We piled into the Jeep and headed over to Duke Medical Center. When we entered his room, he was in a hospital gown, hooked up to an IV. I was both embarrassed and disgusted it had come to this. What was wrong with him?

Ben made the effort to hug him. I was proud of Ben for doing what I could not do.

~*~
Twelve

Journal Entry: *Sometimes, on the drive to the cemetery, I look out the window and spot houses that look friendly. One yellow home is nestled in green pine and has a porch with three white rocking chairs. What would it be like to live inside that house? Would life be peaceful and serene? Is the air inside light and soft, not heavy and stagnant like in our house? The house has a green door, the color of emerald. I bet the people who live there are happy. I hope that they are happy.*
~*~

We attended a Presbyterian church, breaking from the charismatic congregation we were part of when Daniel was alive. The new church had a women's Bible study, and the women in it were kind to acknowledge my sorrow from losing a child. Being accepted felt freeing and wonderful.

But David said I wasn't happy and neither was he. Each day was about putting one foot in front of the other. Taking care of three children, now at ages fifteen, ten, and nine, being involved with their schools, working a new job at a non-profit, and trying to find purpose in this bereaved life didn't give me much time to think about my happiness.

On a Wednesday afternoon while I was at work, David's therapist called to tell me she was considering that he was bipolar. *Considering* seemed like a strange way to put it. Did doctors *consider* someone had cancer? Or a fractured leg? Wasn't it either you had cancer or a broken leg, or you didn't?

"Okay," I said, and waited. What else was she going to share? When I realized she had nothing else to add to the conversation, I ended the call. I prepared for a staff meeting, making copies of a handout our director had asked me to type.

In the meeting, our director talked about a novel program to help our local public schools. I wished I cared for my husband as much as I cared about these handouts I had labored over that morning. *I should know every pill he takes and what it does.* When he'd overdosed three months ago, I should have been more supportive instead of exasperated he was leaving the raising and discipline of our children all on me. When he'd started an extensive CD collection, saying he wanted everything from Bach to Elvis to Queen, and came home with an oak cabinet to house them, I resented him for spending money this way. He was losing jobs and having a hard time finding new ones. This was no time to fritter away money.

As I drove from work to the elementary school to pick up Ben and Liz, I thought about bipolar disorder—what was once known as manic depressive disorder. One of the characteristics of the disease is having days of feeling energetic. David seemed only depressed, sullen. When the kids and I got home, Rachel was already there; she'd gotten a ride from a high school friend. David got home after five, and we ate dinner together. I didn't mention the call from his therapist. I asked if he wanted to play Boggle, but he declined.

~*~

Shortly after Daniel's death, I read a column in the paper by a priest who lovingly wrote about the need to crawl into God's lap, just like children. As I read, my spirit ignited. That's what I needed! I wanted to feel about God as I had before Daniel died. I wrote to the priest. I told him how Daniel had finished his eight-month protocol for neuroblastoma. He was ready to grow his hair back, and then a staph infection found its way into his body, and he plummeted right before the oncology team at the clinic. He coded once he was wheeled to the ER— not once, but twice—and each time was resuscitated. Two EKGs showed only involuntary brain activity, and that was when we made the agonizing decision to take Daniel off the ventilator. We slept in the room with him, praying for a miracle each day. He lived five more days.

In detail, I poured out my frustration with God to this stranger, this newspaper columnist. His response to me was long, but the lines that stood out the most were: *Weep boldly. Hang onto your marriage.*

~*~

When Daniel left us, David and I were thrown into a raging sea where we swam together in hurricane waves. We grabbed what we could to stay afloat. We were going to make it, marriage intact. Then one day, I realized we were no longer swimming together.

When the priest emailed about hanging onto my marriage, I thought, *of course. Nothing's going to happen to it. David and I know how to stay afloat.*

There are some forces greater than the will to hold on.

~*~
Thirteen

David left us in June 2006, after Rachel, Ben, Liz, and I spent a week at Emerald Isle, renting a house on the coast. The week we were away, David started a new computer programming job and had no vacation days, so he couldn't join us for the family beach holiday. We called to chat with him each day.

After a week of sand, sun, and seafood, we returned home. As I pulled the Jeep into the driveway, the kids were eager to see their dad. I noticed his car was gone.

Once we entered the house, our beagle rushed inside through the doggie door, to greet us. An envelope, with my name printed on it, sat on the kitchen table. I opened it to see a five-page letter from David, which explained why he'd had to leave. He loved us but could not live with us anymore as a husband and father.

The kids were in tears as I sat on the sofa in the living room and read their father's letter to them. I knew David had not been well for years.

The morning after David left, I opened the blinds in our bedroom and felt immense freedom.

I was not a prisoner. I was alone now, but not in bondage to alcohol or demons as he was. The sky was a bright June blue, and the cumulus clouds were airy and full of life.

I cried then. For him, for me, for what we'd had. But mostly, I cried because I was free.

The weight of his depression, his drinking, his sadness, and his illness had filled the bedroom we shared. But it had not consumed me. It had not destroyed me.

I would never have left him. I would have stuck with him to avoid divorce. He had said I was unhappy, and then he had said he was unhappy. Since Daniel's death, I didn't know that happiness was possible anymore.

Was I unhappy? Would I be truly happy again? I knew it could never be like before Daniel had died, back when our family had been cohesive and fun.

~*~

I took on the role of the solo parent. Our finances had been stretched, and they would be even tighter with David jobless. I found out from the kids, when they talked with their dad on the phone, he had been fired from his job. Once, he'd had many employers wanting his expertise—Mitsubishi Semiconductors, IBM, ABB, and Progress Energy. But those days were behind him.

When Rachel was two and Daniel was born, David told me my job was much harder than his. I questioned this, since he had to get up each morning to shower, shave, dress in clean clothes, drive to work, and, once there, deal with coworkers and a boss. At least the kids were older now; there were no diapers to change or naps to fuss over.

My boss arranged for me to shift to a full-time position at the non-profit, and I took on part-time jobs on the weekends. My parents gave me generous checks, which covered many of our expenses.

David spent nights in the local Durham Rescue Mission's shelter for the homeless. Some nights, when he didn't make it in line in time for a bed, he slept in his car. When he ended up in South Carolina, his parents arranged for him to get help. He didn't like the rehab program they got him in and left it. He attempted suicide again. In the psych ward, he met a fellow patient and developed a romance with her.

The kids continued to keep up with their father's whereabouts, often through talking with David's parents. Then one afternoon in the fall, David surprised us with a visit. The kids surrounded him with smiles and hugs as he sat on the living room sofa. He smiled, too. He was friendly, similar to his old self. He said he had a job with Lockheed Martin and was moving to Baltimore.

"What good news about the job!" I said.

"Once I start work, I'll be able to send you money." He sounded confident. "I can probably send you a couple hundred each week."

But that never happened. Weeks after he and his new wife moved to Baltimore, she got angry, drove off in their only car, and David attempted suicide again. The doctor at the hospital in Baltimore diagnosed David with bipolar disorder. With a clear diagnosis, I hoped this could be his route to health.

~*~

With David gone, visits to Daniel's Place included just the kids and me. As we tossed the Frisbee one afternoon before a picnic lunch, laughing whenever I missed it, I wondered: If Daniel had not died, would David have spiraled into excessive drinking and abusing medication? If Daniel had survived, would our marriage have survived? I had no strength to go over every detail of my marriage and dissect it. It seemed adapting to life without Daniel and caring for my three earthly children took all my energy. When the Frisbee landed far from us, I ran to pick it up, and then called out to the kids, "Let's eat!"

~*~
Fourteen

After the divorce was final in September 2007, I wondered if there was a man out there who could be my friend. All I needed was a male companion to go out to dinner with me and have adult conversation. I wanted someone to laugh with me while watching a movie. Just every once in a while. Nothing serious. I'd had guy friends in college and in my early twenties; I could have them again as a woman of forty-six. But I would need some help from the internet.

~*~

Sometimes, God responds to our prayers immediately; sometimes, we have to wait. Other times, the answer is no (often the hardest to grasp, especially when we never understand why). And sometimes we don't ask, but God gives.

Carl entered my life via an online "friendship" site. My friend Beth caught me at the computer when she visited and made a comment about me seeking a man to date. I emphasized the need for "only a friend," and she smiled one of those smiles that, when interpreted, means, *You expect me to believe that?*

I did not pray for Carl's arrival as I had for David. Marriage wasn't in my vision or prayers. Carl had grown up in Germany as a military kid; I had grown up in Japan as a missionary kid. We understood how Americans who spent their childhoods overseas feel like foreigners in their own country. Carl was also divorced, and like me, had never wanted the marriage to end. But we both knew willing something does not make it happen.

After hours on the phone (our relationship started out as long-distance until Carl moved from Buffalo to an apartment in Durham) and a few dates, Carl said, "Let's grow old together." I kissed his mustache and told him I was not planning to get old. He smiled. I also told him that while I loved him, I didn't want to be married again. So he stopped the marriage talk, and we enjoyed going out for dinners and being with my kids. We went to Kings Dominion in the summer and camped in the Blue Ridge Mountains in the autumn.

I took Carl to the cemetery to introduce him to our helium-balloon-birthday ritual. I passed out the markers and card stock to the children and handed a marker and card to Carl. I wondered what he'd write. What does one write to a child he's never met but only heard about through stories?

As we drove out of the cemetery grounds, Ben got our attention with, "Hey! What?" Looking out the back seat window, he said, "The sign says Markham Memorial Gardens." He was referring to the white wooden sign at the entrance.

What he said next made us all laugh. "All these years, I thought it was named Daniel's Place."

~*~

The subject of marriage was a constant with Carl. He told me he hoped if he talked enough about wanting to marry me, eventually he'd be able to wear me down. I laughed. I'm a list maker and that includes writing down prayer requests. Wanting to hear from God, the topic of marrying Carl was at the top of the list. We'd been dating eight months when we went Black Friday shopping and entered jewelry stores to look at engagement rings. I tried on a few.

At a New Year's Eve party, I turned to Carl and, above the noise of festivities, said, "2008 was a good year." My first novel, *Rain Song*, was published by Bethany House, and there were book signings, library events, and writing workshops held at conferences. And to top it all off, I'd met Carl.

I leaned in close to him as couples danced in front of us to a song by Chicago.

"What are your hopes for 2009?" I asked.

He pulled out a box from his pocket and opened the lid to expose a familiar-looking diamond ring. "This."

He'd carried the box in his pocket the whole night, and I hadn't suspected a thing!

We got married in Vegas. My first marriage had taken place in a traditional Presbyterian church and had ended up shattered. So this time, I went for something my parents might question.

I had my reasons. Vegas is the kind of place one goes for a no-frills second wedding, and The Little Church of the West, across from The Mandalay Bay Hotel, performed a short and sweet ceremony.

There was much I loved about Carl. His sense of humor matched mine. He listened to me talk about Daniel. He tried his best to get along with Rachel, Benjamin, and Elizabeth. They tried, too. Sometimes, it worked, and other times, it was chaotic. My children get their stubbornness from their mother; I had to learn how to give in and not let every argument be one I needed to win. There is an art to arguing, but we were far from that art. David and I had not developed the art; we'd avoided confrontation. I kept my head in the sand. Carl begged me to take my head out and deal with what needed attention.

~*~
Fifteen

The secondary road that leads from the main road up to the cemetery's slated white fence has a sign that reads, "No Outlet." A funny thought grabbed me as we drove one afternoon, something Daniel might ask—is the sign for those coming to see their loved ones or for those buried there? He and I would have laughed about that, just like we giggled about the man who asked every morning outside the closed hospital room door if we wanted a newspaper. "Newspaper, newspaper, newspaper?"

He was a vendor with a repetition of three. After he asked, I always answered, "No, thank you!"

Daniel and I would wait silently until we heard the salesman move to the next patient's room, inquiring the same way. Only then did Daniel let his giggle loose. When Daniel laughed, I did, too.

His humor—Daniel humor—how I missed sharing laughter with him. My other kids said funny things, they were cute, too. But none of them had talked about *trashing the place* or called a baby in my womb *a raisin*.

~*~

One pilgrimage to the cemetery alone had me asking a question no mother should ever have to ask: "Are you in there?" I stood by Daniel's grave and remembered the day David and I had picked up his ashes from the funeral home. The ashes were inside an urn with a ceramic lamb on the lid. I had been responsible for keeping the urn safe as David drove us across town to the cemetery for the graveside service. At the service, I'd put the urn into the hole that would later be covered with dirt and a stone marker. My question all of these years later was: Had there been ashes inside the urn, or had the funeral home neglected to include any? My reason for this concern started with a single unexpected phone call.

~*~

"Hello?" I answered the phone before the answering machine clicked on.

A woman asked, "Is this Alice Wise-ler?"

"Wisler, yes." Wisler is an unusual surname, often mispronounced. The kids and I were used to that.

"I'm calling from Hall Wynne Funeral Home."

My mind raced. Had a family member died that I didn't know about?

"How are you today?"

"I'm fine," I said with considerable hesitation.

"We have Daniel's ashes here."

"What?"

"Daniel Wisler, we found his ashes when we cleaned a cabinet here."

"But we buried him . . . . He's buried."

"Sometimes there are . . . extras. Would you like them?"

Extra ashes found in a cabinet? How like Daniel to be hiding out in a cabinet for ten years!

"Sure, yes. Yes, I'd like them."

"You can come to pick them up."

"Now?" It was almost time to start making dinner. The kids were home from school and hungry. There were pork chops to bake and a scalloped potato recipe with cheese and onions I wanted to attempt. "Could I come tomorrow?"

"Tomorrow is fine. Have a nice evening."

I felt my insides grow warm and bubbly like I'd just taken a sip of champagne. This was some sort of gift, an unexpected treat. I knew they were only ashes, but the fact that Daniel was still around and someone would have a reason to call me about him was strangely and happily exciting. It had been over ten years since anyone had had a reason to contact me specifically about Daniel.

I removed the pork chops from the fridge and gave them a wide smile. More of Daniel's ashes! My heart danced. We bereaved mamas take whatever we can get.

~*~

When I entered the funeral home the following day, it had a dried-flowers aroma. I introduced myself. "I got a call saying you have my son's ashes here."

Minutes later, I was handed a white cardboard box. The funeral home had placed Daniel's remains inside a clear plastic bag, tied it with a twisty tie, and put the bag inside a box. Daniel Paul Wisler 971223 was printed on a strip of paper taped to the plastic bag. I never knew Daniel had a number. Since I'd never seen or touched cremated human remains, I wasn't sure what the protocol was.

I waited until I got home. The kids were at school; I was alone. I laid the box on the kitchen table and pulled back the lid to expose the plastic bag. "Hello, baby," I said and smiled, amused at how I used the same greeting whenever I went to the cemetery. The next step was to untie the bag, and when I did, I breathed in. Reaching into the bag, I fingered the chalky particles, wondering what part of Daniel I was holding. Was the smooth, gray film inside my palm what had once been his hand?

~*~

Four nights after surgery to insert a double-lumen catheter into Daniel's back, Daniel was dressed for bed in a pair of yellow Loony-Tune hospital pajamas. The lights were out, and he was supposed to be sleeping. Seated in his bed, he started the line-up of jokes he'd memorized from a tattered children's book. "How do you keep an elephant from charging?" he asked. Quickly, he supplied the punch line. "Take away his credit card. How did you find your steak, sir? I looked under the potato and there it was."

"Bedtime, Daniel," I said. Exhausted from a day of procedures and conversing with Dr. Art about what was coming up in the next months for Daniel's protocol, I was ready for sleep.

"Waiter, what's this fly doing in my soup? The backstroke."

Dear God, make him sleep. It was eleven-ten by the clock that hung lopsided against the white wall. The night nurse had made her rounds. The room's one armchair had been stretched out into a bed—sheets, pillows, and blankets all smoothed out. I was on my stomach, under two white blankets, identical to the ones on Daniel's bed. The only way I could sleep (unless I was in the last trimester of pregnancy) was on my stomach.

Daniel slid from the seated position onto his back and looked around the room. "I've been skating since I was two years old!" This time there was a pause before the punch line. "Wow, you must be tired!"

And the jokes kept on coming.

"Aren't you tired, Daniel? Were you this talkative when Daddy spent nights with you?"

"Knock knock. Who's—"

"Daniel! It's time to go to sleep. Honey, please." The chair-bed was parallel to his hospital bed, but sat lower, so I had to look up to see him. When I did, I saw his face lit from the hallway light that crept under the space between the closed door and the floor.

He was smiling, smiling in the near-darkness. It was like he was having a good time at this sleepover. The infusion pump stood on a pole on the other side of his bed, dripping liquid into his line that connected to his catheter. A clear bag hung on the pump's rack. Chemo had started three days ago, but right now, only saline was being infused.

Tomorrow, another drug would be pumped into his catheter. So far, there had been no aversions to any of the medicine.

"Mommy, is the playroom open yet?"

"No. It's bedtime. It's time to go to sleep." He'd had a day of various medicines—most I had trouble pronouncing—fed into him. He had entertained his visitors by handing out Mrs. Grossman stickers, the kind that, when slapped on a surface do not lose their power and droop or curl or do any of those things that stickers of a lesser quality do. He'd enjoyed an afternoon in the playroom. He had not had a nap. Bullfrogs do not sleep, that is a fact we had recently learned, and I was convinced Daniel must be part bullfrog.

"I'm not sleepy." He kicked at the sheet. He must have liked the sound it made because he did it again. And again. "Mommy, can we go to the playroom tomorrow?"

"Yes, now go to sleep."

"I want to play with the train."

I had to admit the train set in the playroom was fascinating. There was one of those wooden tables that stood about three feet off the ground and on top of it sat a mass of tracks and colorful cars. Clearly, it was a Thomas the Tank Engine Train set, and I was probably the only parent in our playgroup who had not given in and bought one for my boys. But I didn't feel like a bad parent; I was just a thrifty one. I had bought a Thomas beach towel for Daniel, which he loved. Of course, he didn't love it as much as he would have loved a train.

I turned over, tried to get comfortable. I might have to opt for sleeping on my side tonight. That way, I could bend my legs at the knees so my feet wouldn't hang off the end of the bed. Whoever designed these beds must hate parents.

"Where's your hand?" Daniel leaned over the bed's railing and into my face.

I lifted a hand for him to see.

He reached down and took it, pulling it over the metal bed railing, as if it were the string to a balloon.

After a few seconds in that position, my arm went numb. There had to be a better way to hold hands. I let go and then weaved my hand through the slats of the railing. This way, my hand could lie on his mattress and not be suspended against the rail.

"A little kiss," he said and planted one on my index finger. He wiggled, tightened his grip. "I'm going to sleep now."

"That's a good idea. Good-night."

A few seconds later: "You know what, Mommy?"

Perhaps if I didn't respond, he'd stop talking. I closed my eyes. He might think I was asleep.

He talked about his brother and his sister, and about going swimming at the neighborhood pool when he got home. He yawned.

I began to lose feeling in my raised arm. The numbness caused me to shift closer to Daniel's bed. I prayed for sleep for him, for both of us. The clock ticked and I counted to fifty, and then, gradually, I let go of his hand. Surely, he was asleep now.

"Mommy!" The sheets rattled with his movement. "Mommy, where's your hand?

"Here, here it is." Reluctantly I reached my hand back toward his. He found it, wrapped his little fingers into it, and that was when I decided sleep was not going to be an option for me. To make the hand-holding more comfortable, I turned onto my side.

At midnight, I heard a change in Daniel's breathing and hoped that was the sound of sleep. Slowly, I released my thumb. Since that went well, I pulled a finger loose, then another. Soon my hand was away from his. This time there was no response. He was in dreamland.

~*~

A few years after my marriage to Carl, he suggested I take some of the ashes on our trip out West. We were going to the Grand Canyon and had a boat trek scheduled on the Colorado River. I put some of Daniel's ashes inside a medicine bottle and carried them in my purse through security, onto our flights, and then in the rental when we drove from Las Vegas to Arizona. When Daniel debated where to go on his Make-a-Wish trip, he and I took the elevator to the sixth floor of the hospital. In a waiting room, we'd looked at photos in National Geographic of the Southwest, the reds, the canyons, the bold colors.

"How about a hot air balloon ride over the desert?" I'd suggested, pointing at a yellow and white balloon suspended against a blue sky. I'd turned the page to photos of a dude ranch. Horses stood inside a fence.

"What do you do at a dude ranch?" Daniel had asked me.

"I really don't know," I'd said. "But the horses look friendly."

~*~

Now I would let some of his ashes flow into the Colorado River. Carl, Ben, Liz, and I were on a small motorboat at the bottom of the Grand Canyon, where the Colorado meanders. Before the tour boat started, I stepped away from the others. Quietly, I went to one of the railings, stooped down, and ran a hand into the water. The air was 120 degrees Fahrenheit, but the water, I later learned, was a mere 50 degrees. I unscrewed the cap on the bottle I had clenched in my right hand. And then, I turned the bottle upside down and let the gray ashes meet the water.

Earlier, Carl had reminded me that the Colorado swims into the Pacific Ocean, and once Daniel got there, he'd be everywhere. I knew Daniel didn't care about his ashes, and I knew he was doing all the great things Heaven holds, but for me, the thought of Daniel floating into the ocean and teeming through the waves with sea creatures was a mighty image.

~*~

Sixteen

Daniel swimming in the Colorado was a happy thought, albeit a mild one compared to his spirit living in heaven with Jesus. But I had to deal with the earthly issues I faced at home. These consisted of Carl wanting to start a woodworking business, and I wasn't sure what my role in that would be, and Ben and Liz and their teenaged antics.

After dropping Liz and Ben off at their part-time jobs, I did laps at local parks. I took up walking, and I walked four miles nearly every day for three years. It helped to get out and be in nature when things were stressful at our house, where emotions and attitudes loomed, and I, as the mom, and Carl, as the stepdad, were often at odds on how to raise and discipline the kids.

When I walked the perimeter a few times to get my four miles at Daniel's Place, I asked God for help with our family. There had been a time when all I'd done was petition God. Then Daniel died, and I held off on asking God for anything. I wrestled with the concept of prayer. It took years to discover I had a limited view of prayer because I had a limited view of God.

As I exercised, I noted the holly bushes, bouquets of fresh flowers on grave tops, and the scarlet cardinals in the juniper tree. God's magnificent creation was all around me, and it filled me with peace. "Let me focus on your magnitude," I cried. "Let my problems have a lesser hold on me than the truth, which is that you love me, you are for me, and you will never leave (even when you are silent). I belong to you."

~*~

When the children were small, they liked to hike up to the mausoleum with David. I went once and was not a fan. The building smelled of mildew and old socks, and with a green wall-to-wall outdoor carpet that was damp, those smells stayed embedded.

One day, the mausoleum looked inviting, so I decided to enter and see what I might find. The glass door was unlocked, and I ambled inside. No one was there; I'd never seen anyone there. I noted the grave plaques on the walls. Some held sprigs of flowers. Then I sat on one of the white wooden pews and observed the stained-glass window before me. I had never seen any service performed in this room, but something came over me, and having one of my own seemed like a noble idea. For some reason, this service started with a song. Softly at first, I sang the words to a familiar tune.

"Thank you, Lord, for saving my soul. Thank you, Lord, for making me whole. Thank you, Lord, for giving to me thy great salvation so rich and free." It didn't sound too bad, and I knew it was because the acoustics were superb in this room. So, seated among the dead, bodies in urns in the walls, I belted the song out again. And again. I was thankful to God for sending Jesus, the gift of salvation and life. I wanted gratitude to be my mantra. After one more round, I took my phone and recorded my singing. I sent a copy to Rachel. The next time she was at Daniel's Place, she entered the mausoleum and sang a song she liked.

No one complained about either of our voices. The dead don't complain, so we continued freely singing among them. When Carl and I went to Daniel's Place with our boxer, Bella, on Mother's Day, a few women gathered around a grave near Daniel's. They sang in loud voices all the verses to the 1915 song, *Mother*. The chorus they repeated half a dozen times. "M is for the million things she gave me, O means that she's only growing old, T is for the tears she shed to save me, H is for her heart of purest gold. E is for her eyes with love-light shining, R means right and right she'll always be. Put them all together, they spell mother, a word that means the world to me."

I wanted to tell them about the mausoleum and that, perhaps, they would like to try the acoustics in that part of the cemetery, but instead, I breathed a breath of relief when they got in their vehicles and left.

The cemetery was quiet again. Sparrows flew from tree limb to limb. The cemetery hawk swooped low over the verdant landscape.

It may be time to come up with a better song to honor moms.

~*~

Seventeen

You never know what will wake you in the morning—a reminder of something you forgot to do the day before, a cherished memory that rests against your chest, or a word that turns into a call to action. I woke on a foggy summer morning with the word *Go* in my mind. I dressed, left Carl a note, and drove to the cemetery.

I arrived at the sloping green grounds dotted with assorted flowers. I walked to the tiny slab of stone my children and I have grown to love. There, I gave one of my usual greetings: "Hey, honey." Sometimes, the greeting was: "Hi, baby." Other times, I wanted to say my son's name, since I never got to hear it enough. Taking a lemon-scented wet wipe, I cleaned my son's marker of bird poop and brushed away twigs so his name and dates were clear.

Continuing the rituals I'd developed over the years, I strolled across the grass, pausing to read familiar epitaphs. Peregrina, a beloved mother and grandmother, had an armload of fresh red roses in the vase on her stone. The cemetery hawk circled overhead—most likely looking for a critter to surprise—but I rather liked to think he was protecting the gravestones. I watched as he showed off his wing span.

We have rituals because they help us make sense of life and give us a sense of control. Coffee in the morning, a glass of wine in the evening, chocolate cakes on birthdays, barbeques with friends when the days last longer. At the cemetery, walking among the tombstones and often settling on Daniel's Thomas the Tank Engine towel to write had become serene and holy actions for me.

Solomon's grave was new to me and drew me in. The scripture passage on his marker was well known: *I have finished my course. I have kept the faith.* The line from 2 Timothy 4:7 quotes a version of the Bible that reads "*my* course," not "*the* course."

My first response to this stranger's epitaph was, "Well, Solomon, you had 75 years, so the passage makes sense to put on your resting place." Daniel, Audrey, and Taylor only got a little time.

Images of Daniel cycled through my mind. There was the day he wore a *Jesus Loves You* pin to the hospital and said that Jesus was his friend. Once, he told me that you give gifts to your friends, so he handed out stickers to his. When we crossed the mile-high swinging bridge at Grandfather Mountain during a family vacation, he held my hand because I am afraid of heights. I saw his little face and the way it lit up when his siblings entered his hospital room or when I bought a watermelon.

From memory, I recited another part of the verse. *I have fought the good fight.* Or, to put it in Solomon's style: *I have fought my good fight.*

As a cancer patient, Daniel had fought through rounds of chemotherapy, surgeries, radiation treatments, infections, and invasive needles.

I stood immobilized for a few minutes. Then I walked back to Daniel's spot. "You were created for a purpose, and you lived it," I said. "I don't know why you had to leave for heaven at four years old, but your life was every bit as profound as someone who got to live to see 75 or 85 or 92."

The mist still hovered; there was no burst of sunlight, no sound of angel wings or trumpets, absolutely no physical indication I'd had an epiphany. But I knew God had spoken to me through the words on Solomon's grave, and the comfort of the scripture verse would stay with me.

A tear slipped down my cheek. I labeled it gratitude.

Gratitude works through the hardness of heartache and provides something to hold onto besides sorrow. Gratitude is a respite from questioning and contemplating. It's like a dance that takes your spirit and sets it free.

~*~

While bereaved parents stood in the hallway at one of the bereavement conferences, I talked with a woman who told me that if her son hadn't died the way he did, something else would have killed him. Her son had died at age seventeen in a two-car accident. She said it was his time to go. If it hadn't been for the accident, he would have died another way. Perhaps he would have died from cancer, or a heart problem. When she told me this, I had to make a point not to stare at her with my mouth wide open. Mothers who had lost a child to a car accident felt something should have happened to keep their child alive. But this mother calmly said, "It was his time to go." I wondered when she had come to terms with his death this way. How long had it taken? Was her faith in God so deep she trusted there was nothing she could have done to keep her son, her precious boy, from experiencing his last breath? Maybe she was right. At the time, I was more interested in getting to the restroom before my writing workshop started than trying to figure out her rationale.

I remembered her words over the following years. I wanted to ask her if she still felt the same way and if perhaps it was because she trusted God has a plan for each of us and that when our days are up, we can do nothing to prolong them. But I'd lost touch with her. I couldn't even recall her name.

~*~

Daniel's life was only meant to be—ordained, commissioned, designed—for four years and almost six months. Nothing I could have done would have prolonged his days. While I would never understand why he had to die, I would focus on a remarkable joy, which was: For some undeserving reason, I got to be his mama.

~*~
Eighteen

I told Rachel about Solomon. She watched my eyes grow teary as she nodded with understanding. Even though I had learned much about the cemetery from strangers' epitaphs, I still had shame about Daniel's last days creep into my mind. I couldn't shake it. I read in the book of Philippians about renewing your mind and filling it with thoughts of excellence and purity. But the guilt demon lingered.

Guilt is perhaps the most painful companion to death, wrote Elisabeth Kubler-Ross, famous for her study on death and dying.

Of course, I knew I had not physically harmed my son or brought about his death. But a mother's guilt is not rational. Ever since the beginning of time, mamas have had this complex of believing the lie that it's all up to them. If a child gets a DUI, crashes the car, forgets his homework, or gets an illness, it is Mama's fault, or if not her fault, at least she should have been able to keep it from happening. In the bereavement support group meetings, there was a stream of love and yearning but also a thick coat of guilt. The guilt masked the desperation for forgiveness. Guilt was talked about often, but forgiveness? Not as much. Mamas are tough, both in the animal kingdom and among humans. We enjoy the closeness of our children and the feeling we have taught them well and are strong enough to protect them from the world. We mamas want to believe we can keep everyone safe—just because we will it, just because that is the way our hearts are built.

When Daniel was first hospitalized, I had asked Dr. Art how a three-year-old gets a malignant tumor. I went back over my pregnancy. Each "event" I presented to Daniel's oncologist received the same response.

Me: "I had a sinus infection (the only one I have ever had) when I was seven months pregnant. My OBGYN doctor gave me a prescription for something, I can't recall what, to cure it. Did that cause Daniel's cancer?"

Dr. Art: "No."

Me: "I was eight months pregnant at the beach, and I got food poisoning at a restaurant, could that have caused the cancer?"

Dr. Art: "No."

Me: "It was really bad. I threw up and had diarrhea—both at the same time."

Dr. Art showed sympathy but shook his head.

Me: "David and I got hepatitis A after Daniel was born. We both turned yellow. That must have been the culprit!"

Dr. Art: "No."

Me: "What caused it?" (I had asked this question before, but thought it should be repeated.)

Dr. Art: "We don't know."

Which meant, if nobody knew, then it was nobody's fault. Our family adopted the mantra: *It's nobody's fault.*

Daniel found me crying in my bedroom one afternoon after he'd spent his first week on the oncology ward. His words of comfort to me were, "It's nobody's fault, Mommy."

~*~

When Daniel's death date fell on a Sunday, Carl and I drove into Wake County, took some winding roads, and happened upon some woods. We stopped, parked, and ventured deep into the clusters of trees. There was an abandoned cabin, shed, tall pines, and the stuff postcards of North Carolina are made of. We walked. I wanted to find a quaint coffee shop, but the woods were thick, and the abandoned cabin looked like it had not had anyone drinking coffee in it for years. I was more aware of signs and gestures on this day than other days, and I felt open to God's presence. I observed the scents in the air, the foliage, the sounds of birds, and the sorrow of my longing. After we trekked, found the road, and made it back to our vehicle, we got into the Jeep and drove home.

I knew we would never be able to find those woods again, since we had just happened upon them and hadn't written down any of the names of the winding roads that got us there. So we have not been back.

Years later, Daniel's death date was a Sunday again. I could have stayed home from church. I considered it. There had never been any pressure to spend this day well, be productive, or come up with something grand. At the end of the day, I was the only one who would know how I got through. I was the one with no expectations. It's a no-lose-no-win situation. Disaster had already marked this day and the days leading up to it for me. In the early years after Daniel's death, this date had been only about survival.

The rest of the country enjoyed the tradition of men in black top hats holding up an overweight groundhog they've named Punxsutawney Phil. Would this creature see his shadow? Would there be six more weeks of winter or an early spring?

~*~

February 2, 2020, was three days away. Getting through the day had been the motto in the past. But this year, I had something I needed to do. I made plans.

The Dollar Tree was a popular place that Sunday afternoon. The check-out lines stretched to the end of the aisles. A gentleman in a cap held the door for me. The first thing I saw after thanking him and entering were the lines and then, to my left, the two Mylar balloons. A blue star balloon dangled next to a Happy Birthday one. I pulled on the string of the star balloon just to test it out. The criteria were simple: It must be able to fly. It also must fly with a piece of paper attached to its string. I could have grabbed the star balloon then, but I didn't. If it was really mine, if this balloon was the one to carry out the ritual that afternoon, it would still be there swaying near the counter when I came back for it, when I was ready. If someone purchased it while I strolled down the aisles looking for those nuts I liked, I'd have one of the clerks pump helium into another balloon for me. And if their pump was broken, as it had been once before when I came to buy a balloon, I would be grateful for the shiny star balloon and consider it a gift that it was waiting for me. This logic made sense to me.

Minutes later, I was in line with nine customers ahead of me. People had buggies and baskets filled with paper plates, cookies, boxes of Valentine's chocolate, jars of condiments, and oven mitts. You can get anything you want at the Dollar Tree. As I looked around, I wanted to sing a line or two from Arlo Guthrie's song, "Alice's Restaurant." But I was not that bold.

I hadn't picked up a basket, so my hands were filled with a butterfly lawn ornament and three of my favorite packets of mixed nuts. One pack had cranberries, raisins, and cashews. Two held sugared walnuts. I had selected cards for friends from church who were in sad stages of life. One had recently lost a spouse, and finding a suitable card was no easy feat. When Daniel died, I extensively studied sympathy cards by perusing various grocery and drug stores. Most cards were sappy or overly religious; there were few that were compassionate and empathetic.

At last, it was my turn to check out. I remembered to tell the cashier I wanted a balloon. The woman in front of me had already told him she needed two. He handed her change and then called out to his co-worker to tell her to come out and blow up two balloons. "Deborah, we need you out here," he hollered.

"Give me a minute, Matt," she shouted from a back room.

The woman in front wanted matching bright pink balloons with Happy Birthday. She looked at the wall behind the balloon counter where the flat Mylar shells were lined up, each with a printed number.

I saw the star balloon against the wall with the number eight. When it was my turn, and Matt had rang up the packs of nuts, I told him I also wanted a balloon. "Number eight."

The woman behind me said, "I want ten balloons."

Matt expelled an audible sigh. It was a sigh that, if it could speak, would say, "Really, ten balloons? You expect us to blow up ten balloons for you on this busy day?" Turning to me, he handed me my bag of purchases and said his co-worker would be right with me. She appeared from wherever she'd been and was busy caring for another cashier who needed dollars or a roll of quarters or something. I wasn't paying attention to what the cashier required because I was under the balloon—the shiny, blue, star balloon, the one that was still available. I knew then the balloon was waiting for me.

I tugged on the string. "Can I just take this one?" I asked Matt, who had left his register and was by my side. He took hold of the white string and transferred it to me. He was most likely relieved one less balloon had to be blown up.

Outside, the wind wanted to take the balloon from me, but I held tight. I wrangled it into my Jeep and tied the string to the seat belt in the back. I spoke to it the way I talked to innate objects. "Don't fly away here. It's not time yet." As I spoke, I could see it had life in it. I had no idea when it was blown up, but I knew if I let it loose, it would fly. We drove, the balloon and I, toward Old Chapel Hill Road, and then I made a left turn at Farrington. Minutes later, we had arrived.

~*~

Decades earlier, a hospital social worker told me perhaps I needed to forgive myself for real or imagined guilt.

But, as the expression goes, that was easier said than done. Maybe I was scared I might discover Daniel's death was my fault. It was one thing to say it was my fault and carry the burden of guilt; it was another to pin it on me. Like when you keep saying you're fat or your feet are big, and everyone says, "No, no, you're not overweight, and your feet aren't too big." But deep down, you know you're chubby and have wide feet. But if people start agreeing with you and say, "Well, yeah, you're right, you are pudgy, and your feet remind me of elephant ears," then you begin to fear. I wanted someone—ideally, God—to tell me Daniel's death wasn't my fault. I wanted him to send an angel like Gabriel who appeared to Mary or to speak to me in a dream as he'd spoken to Joseph. *Alice, Daniel did not die because you didn't know you were supposed to take him to the hospital. Daniel's time was up. He was only supposed to live four years. You did not have control over when he was to be born, and you did not have control over when he was to die.* If I had been given this message from God, perhaps I could have stashed my guilt under a stone and soldiered on.

But God did not come to me in a dream or via an angel's message, so I had to eliminate the blame alone.

On an afternoon when the house was calm, and I felt a little bold, I took out my journal. I wrote the date. I always date entries. And then I began a letter to Daniel.

I am sorry that I was looking to the healing and unaware (naïve) of what was happening to your body that Tuesday, January 22, night. I was so focused on God watching out for you and naïve about what could happen. I should have taken you in that night. I should have called and gone to the ER. They would have admitted you when I told them you had diarrhea. I know they would have. And if the infection, which was most likely brewing then, still raged on, they would have given you a blood transfusion. You could have had a chance at fighting the infection because your counts would have gone up, and had the staph aureus infection done its damage, your body could have had more vitality to combat it. Instead of death, perhaps you'd only be dealing with a damaged heart. I have gone around in circles for nine months. The last piece— the extreme guilt—I cannot let go. So . . . I am asking you to forgive me, and I will have to forgive myself.

The letter had been my assignment twenty years ago. Had I forgiven myself back then? Had I realized mamas do not hold the control they think they have?

There was still work to do.

~*~
Nineteen

"Hello, baby," I said when I arrived. "I bet you're surprised to see me today. I know it's not a day I usually come here, but sometimes new things must be done to eliminate the old things that bog us down." The wind whipped around me, blowing my hair into my eyes.

After finishing my little speech, I looked out over the familiar scene of rows of graves with swaying flowers.

Inside the warmth of the Jeep, I took out a pen and a sheet of memo paper. I wrote *No Guilt, Just Love. I love you, Daniel. ~Mommy*. I cut a tiny hole and slipped the white string through with a pair of scissors I'd packed. I knotted the balloon's string to the paper.

With caution, I took the star balloon outside as it bounced against me, ready to fly. I stood by Daniel's grave as I had many times before. I thought of the first time I'd seen his gravestone and how disappointed I'd been with the size. I was glad that regret had faded. Now, other regrets needed to go, too.

I saw him at the beach with his arms spread wide as he took in the beautiful June day. Earlier, I'd posted the beach photo on my Facebook page with the caption:

This is how you experience the ocean: Fill your fists with sand from the beach; throw back your shoulders; stand with your face to the sun; squint; smile; listen to the waves; know you are loved; gratitude. Longing and love never fade, only grow, and so does gratitude for the treasure of this Wild Boy, this Brave Cookie.

Susan commented how she would never forget him. His Mother's Morning Out teacher added sweet lines about him. A church nursery worker, who had cared for him back when I had to sneak out of the room before he realized I was leaving, wrote that she loved him. Teresa let me know she still had Daniel's photo on her fridge. I thought about how I'd been fearful no one would remember him.

I imagined him in his heavenly state as radiant, healthy, and perfect. I remembered the first poem I ever wrote at the cemetery and the beauty that entered my grief when I thought about him experiencing heaven and the glory of angels and Jesus.

~*~

On the last day of Daniel's life, my mom read him a story from a book the playroom worker had brought to his room. It was about a little boy who had found a star. He took the star and kept it in his room. But the star's light began to fade. As it dimmed, the boy knew he had to let the star return to where it belonged, back up to the sky. Mom finished the book and said to Daniel, lying silently in his hospital bed, "And Daniel, you can go, too. You can go up to Heaven."

Within minutes, the monitors hooked up to Daniel buzzed and beeped. David and I were called into his room. Daniel was about to leave earth and sail up to his eternal home.

~*~

I held the balloon string tightly and recalled the first time we'd sent dozens of balloons into the sky on the first birthday without Daniel. I had not wanted to let my balloon go, because that meant what was real was real—I had a dead child and, therefore, a need to have a memorial birthday. I didn't want to be that mama. And now, on a Sunday, the same day of the week Daniel had died, I was able to let go of the string. When the star balloon skirted across the lawn, it went in a different direction than any other balloon we had sent up. It went east.

"Oh, Daniel," I said as I watched the balloon travel, "look at how forgiveness rises and fills the sky. Look how far shame and guilt blow away."

It was my graveyard ceremony, a service of freedom and forgiveness for one. But it felt like I had broken through with the vigilance of an army of hundreds. The balloon sailed further from me until it was a dot in the vast sky. I smiled into the sunlight. When the balloon had vanished, I added my small benediction of gratitude. "Thank you, God. Thank you."

I love you, Daniel.

And that is what I want to remember the most.

~*~

Twenty-six years after Daniel's death, on February 2, Rachel sent a text to her siblings and me: *Happy Daniel's Day everyone! It can be a celebration, if you so choose.*

Yes, yes, I so choose!

~*~
Twenty

Once more at the Dollar Tree, days before yet
another birthday without him, I bought a large,
green, garden pinwheel. At the grave, I added some
watermelon stickers to the round blades. I forgot
who had sent the stickers, but I had kept them in a
drawer with other watermelon mementoes. I stuck
the pinwheel in the ground by Daniel's marker and
watched the wind spin the blades. The simple things
done in memory can bring the most comfort and
peace.

That Independence Day in the hospital with the
leftover watermelon would always make me smile.

How about the bathtub?

Why not?

The wind paused; I waited for it to take the
blades on another circular journey.

Later, ambling along the rows, I noted other
lawn ornaments of loved ones displayed on
gravestones. Some were fancy—butterfly and

dragonfly solar lights. I passed a birdhouse on a pole trimmed in vines and then walked over to read Taylor's epitaph. *We're so glad you came.* The words held so much meaning each time I saw them.

A brief life does not mean a life without purpose.

I wrote about Taylor in my journal, all those questions I had for his parents, whom I would most likely never meet. My journal kept me sane. Author Alice Walker wrote that writing saved her and that the lives we save are our own when we write. A plaid journal that had a snap to close it was what I used to write about Daniel's diagnosis. But it was after his death that journaling took on a new life. Survival. The journal didn't judge me, tell me to shut up, or criticize my grammar. I could write whatever I wanted, and no one had to read it.

When I fretted about how my children would turn out being raised by a sorrowful mama, I wrote. When Rachel had a hard time sleeping because she was afraid someone might be dead when she woke, I comforted her, and then when she settled, I left her room to write.

The passing of time did lessen my intense pain; time can be a healer. But the underlining aches from not having Daniel present in our lives lingered. Just as scars are still visible years later, the effect of his death will be with me always. My world had changed, my faith had taken a beating, and my prayer life had altered. I had expected God to move in one way, and for whatever reason, he had other plans for Daniel.

~*~

I'd planned to write a book about Daniel, and yet, each time I try, I don't get far. How do I write about a boy who sat on my sciatic nerve for three months, memorized a joke book, and took his last breath in my lap? How do I tell what his short life and death taught me? How do I cram all this into the pages? Where does this story of over two decades begin? I know it has no end.

I will start at Daniel's Place, the grassy field of tombstones. Peregrina, Audrey, Solomon, Colin, Taylor, and others are there, too, so technically, it is also their place. I did not know them. But my son, Daniel, was born of my body and is still connected to my heart. We are still woven, like one seamless fabric.

Six months after Daniel died, I did a naive thing. I sent pages of my journal to an editor, hoping he would like them. He wrote back: *You need more time. You need more perspective. It's too early to tell this story.*

I thought he was unkind to reject me. But over the years, I realized he had saved me from embarrassment. We don't need our scribbling published. There is something to be said for waiting to tell a story instead of trying to understand how you handle your experiences while they are happening. He was right. In the beginning, all I had was pain, confusion, and heartache. That was what bled onto the pages. No one wants to read woe-is-me paragraphs. Readers want to know that although your heart felt punctured and your mind was going crazy with guilt at 2 a.m. for not saving your child, you dealt with the situation. You didn't stay in the miry pit. You decided to seek God. While you struggled, you cried. You refused to ask God for anything; you stopped praying. You wanted a god who would fit inside your pocket, one you could control. You opened the Bible, found God, chalked God up to being mysterious, and learned how to pray. You discovered a deeper faith, went to the cemetery, listened, and learned how to embrace the beauty of being a child of God once again.

~*~

Expectation—the disciples and the Jews expected their Messiah to overthrow the government. But he didn't. Instead, he was captured with the kiss of betrayal and put to death. Wow, talk about circumstances not turning out as expected! Even though they were with him eating, praying, walking, fishing, and conversing, the disciples didn't know him as deeply as we might think they would have. They saw him in the temple, and they saw the miracles he performed, yet they still had doubts. What they expected, possibly even what they had been taught by their parents and grandparents about what to expect of a Messiah, was not someone like Jesus. What they expected and what occurred were at opposite ends. John the Baptist, the preparer of the way for Jesus, was in prison. When his disciples approached Jesus, they were doubtful. In Luke 7:20, it's written that they said, "John the Baptist sent us to you to ask, 'Are you the one who is to come, or should we expect someone else?'"

In the devastation of my grief, I also asked Jesus, "How can you be the One?"

"Lord, to whom would we go?" Peter replied when Jesus asked if he and the others would leave him. "You have the words of eternal life. We believe and know that you are the Holy One of God."

Days later, when Jesus was before Pilate, and it looked like Jesus was going to die, Peter feared. When he was asked by a servant girl if he was with Jesus, he panicked. Peter was not ready to die, too. So, this friend, who had confessed his faithfulness to the Holy One of God, walked on water to him, asked him to not only wash his feet, but all of him, denied knowing him.

"Woman, I do not know him." He was asked again and once more, each time stressing he had no association with Jesus Christ.

There's a rooster in my neighborhood, and, each morning, it lets the neighborhood know that he's alive, crowing, ready for a new day. Often, I think of Peter and his fear when I hear the animal. I think of how Jesus predicted Peter would pretend to not know him. "Before the rooster crows today," Jesus told his disciple, "you will deny me three times."

I hear my own cries when that neighborhood rooster sounds his. *Oh, Jesus, I won't deny you. Not me. I trust you. I love you.* And then . . . . Calamity happened. The winds and waves exploded. Things didn't go as planned. *Where are you, Jesus?*

I look forward to seeing Peter in heaven; we have so much in common. On earth, he was someone who could be as fickle as I can be when the dark clouds cause me to doubt and stray from the One who has the words of eternal life.

~*~
Twenty-one

Being lost between the lines has never won my confidence.

I bought a notebook with geraniums on the cover, wrote a few lines, drank some German beer, wrote into the early morning, and felt energized, vibrant, and young. The next day, I woke with a headache and read the pages in the notebook, and the only thing I was thankful for was that I had not typed them up and sent them to an editor.

The next time I tried was on my new laptop. I drank imported Italian red wine from a crystal glass and put on some Phil Collins. The music from the *Tarzan* soundtrack brought out the hidden muse. I typed all night and, with each sip of wine, knew I was onto something. But weeks later, when I opened the file at Daniel's Place, the story that should have felt like an expression of love had the opposite effect. Instead of embracing it, I wanted to hurl the laptop across the cemetery. Over all those gravestones. My storytelling voice was off. Did I have to sound so woeful? Where was my humor?

"Perhaps he was right. You know who I mean," I said, as I sat by Daniel's marker. "That editor who rejected my story decades ago. He said then it was too soon. He said I needed perspective. At that time, I shouted, 'What does he know?'"

Twenty years later, something told me there had been time to weed out the anger and agony, especially the sentimental sap, and write what I knew. Make it work. Slice it up so others could dig their fingers around it and take bites.

I still wasn't sure how to begin. Did I go over all the details of Daniel's diagnosis and demise? I had volumes written after we were given the results of the EEG, and my reaction to hearing the words that tore me apart: my son's brilliant brain was only operating at an involuntary level. Did I start with a fun memory of when he and I watched a train rumble down the tracks at the park?

At least I could have the ability to tell the story I'd missed coffee dates for, the story that left me weepy and loved, sensitive and bold. I knew the sequences; they sounded much better in my mind than anywhere else.

Whenever Carl and I watched movies dealing with grief and loss, I felt tugs at my heart. If the actress or actor portrayed their bereaved character well, my thoughts took over: *I could write that, I should write something true and honest about lament. I know the depth of loneliness.* My thoughts often caused me to miss parts of the movie.

Sadly, the meaningful tale I expected to develop on the pages inside my computer was not there. Those pages I had typed only yawned at me, and there were late nights when even the cursor refused to blink.

I put the story aside and focused on our woodworking business—the customers, sanding products, preparing orders for shipment. I wished I didn't want to tell my story, to create pages of epiphany with purpose. I wished I could be satisfied with letting go of a vow I'd made at the grave about writing a book.

~*~

Valentine's Day 1998 had been cloudy. David and I gave chocolates to each other. On Valentine's ten years earlier, we'd had our first date at a restaurant in Osaka. David had tipped over a glass of red wine by accident, and, as the liquid ran across the white linen tablecloth, the wait staff rushed over to our table to sop it up. Embarrassed, David had said, "We're going to remember this for a long time."

That year after Daniel's death, the memory of our first Valentine's didn't hold its usual glow of nostalgia. Although we wrote sentiments of love on cards to each other, the sense of well-being was missing. Nothing was going to feel normal again. Rachel drew a big heart on a sheet of construction paper and included all six of our names—Daddy, Mommy, Rachel, Daniel, Benjamin, and Elizabeth—all together in one spot, the way they belonged.

At the Dollar Tree that Saturday morning, we chose one heart balloon printed with *I Love You* and headed to Daniel's Place. We wrote on folded note cards the leftover ones from Daniel's birthday, ones I had punched holes in the corners. The holes made it easy to put the balloon strings through, loop, tie, and send. I used the side of the van as a table to write my love letter to Daniel.

Ben and Liz scribbled messages I was sure Daniel could translate into: *Where are you? We hear about you almost every day and play with your trucks and dinosaurs, but where are you*? David wrote for about three minutes; I wondered what he had to say. I knew he wore guilt like a heavy shroud around his shoulders. That shroud was heavier than what I wore. I knew he was not the type to forget or forgive the past. The last night Daniel had at home, David had begged his son to shut up. We all wanted sleep, but Daniel had been awake making trips to the bathroom and talking.

Rachel added stickers to her note and placed Winnie-the-Pooh and Toy Story stickers on Daniel's marker next to his name. We slipped the balloon's string through the holes, five cards strung together, love on paper. David tied the end of the line to form a knot. We stood in a circle as David held the lone balloon against the wind. "We love you, Daniel!" we cried in unison as David let the balloon go. The balloon wobbled, a slow start. It shimmied a few feet to the left and traveled along the ground. It looked like our *I Love You* would not make it to heaven.

"It's too heavy," said David. He chased after it, captured it, and returned it to where we waited. We would have to improvise.

He untied the string, and I pulled off the five note cards.

"Let's just all sign one card," I suggested. The next time we planned to send up only one balloon and wanted five notes attached, we'd need to use lighter paper.

We signed one card. David attached it to the string. Then he cut the line with his van key to decrease the weight even more. Another knot, and it looked ready.

Once more, we hovered over the balloon near Daniel's grave. David let go of the string. We watched the wind take the balloon up into the gray sky. This time it worked.

We stood shivering in the February air. When we could no longer see the balloon, we got into our dusty emerald van and headed home.

~*~

As I recalled the balloon story from Valentine's decades before, I started to chop. I cut out the sweet Daniel stories only a mother could love. Many didn't add to the themes I was trying to accomplish. I wrote notes to myself about how to format my book. I cut it down to the bare bones, as they say. It became a simple recipe, like a loaf of plain white bread. There were no raisins, rye flour, or diversion from the basic bread recipe I had used before. My bread was simplistic, not elaborate like the recipes on Bread Week Carl and I watched on the *Great British Baking Show*.

I got the bare bones down—the diagnosis, his death, and how the first cookbook I'd compiled in memory of many children came about—but something was missing. The bread needed some pizzazz to it, some zing. How did I know what to add if I didn't know what kind of bread I expected? What did I expect? What did I want?

Over two decades ago, I had promised to remember Daniel in a big way. I thought of the books we'd read together in his hospital room. In addition to *Pierre*, there had been all of the *Curious George* stories, *The Cat in the Hat*, *Where the Wild Things Are*, and *Go, Dog. Go!* The messages in each book were important. For me, as an author, a book was my way.

I had a plain loaf of bread, no frills. I added my faith to it. I sounded preachy. In my published novels, I never preached. I toned it down. This was not a sermon. One afternoon, I sat beside the grave with a cup of sweet iced tea from Bojangles and a salad with a hint of dressing and asked the sky: What am I doing?

I read a quote by Maya Angelou: *There is no greater agony than bearing an untold story inside you.* Maya was dead, buried in Winston-Salem, NC, although I also read her ashes were scattered. Maya was everywhere now. I read quotes to inspire me. Quotes by Ernest Hemingway and David Thoreau filled my Pinterest Writing Workshop page.

What was a story about a brave boy without anecdotes about who he was? The story was nothing without tossing in the Daniel stories, so I picked a few. I would select two or three, the way one picks out the two or three best potatoes or apples for a recipe. I had nearly five-hundred stories, so this would be an arduous task.

Carl knew I was struggling and wrote a note for my desk: *Do not give up.* Then one day, he said, "Put it aside. And as you put it aside, you will get more the feel for the story." As I baked peanut butter cookies and fruit cobbler, recipes from three of the memorial cookbooks I had compiled, memories of Daniel came to me, and the tone and voice in which I wanted to write the scenes began to sound in my mind.

~*~

If I wanted to write about Daniel's life, there was no better book to read than the journal I had kept during his diagnosis. Yet I was unsure. What would I find on those pages? How would my 55-year-old self deal with the 35-and 36-year-old? Would I like her? Would I approve of what she said and did?

On a brave day, I sat in one of Grandma's recliners I had inherited at her death, and opened my journal, fondly known as Picnic Plaid.

I found him on the pages of my journal. He appeared that spring when we listened for the train's rhythmic whistle together at the park. I found him under the weeping willow, on the coast where sand and waves play forever, and on the swinging bridge at Grandfather Mountain. He was the only kid I'd ever known who fell onto a prized pig at a petting zoo, and was bitten. (The owner was summoned by the zoo personnel, but never showed up.)

Then there was the time Daniel stamped his legs. Only wearing a blue and white striped shirt and a pair of white big boy pants, Daniel sat on the hallway floor, his legs covered in a blue self-inking thank you stamp. He was three, before surgery, before cancer, before he named himself Brave Cookie.

When I saw him stamped, I pulled the camera out of the kitchen drawer and snapped a picture. After that, I made him pose. He remained on the floor, and then I suggested he move to the stairs where the light was better. He smiled, one of his I-know-I've-done-wrong-but-ain't-I-cute smiles. I got another picture. He smiled again. What a kid. What a silly, happy, wonderful boy.

And this is how I remember him, his humor, his smile, the way he held my hand in the nights between the slats of the hospital bed. He no longer clung to me like the proverbial boy tied to his mama's apron strings because he was well beyond his years by the time he was four. Months before he left, he told me that "heaven is a good place to stay." And when he took that last breath in my arms, I hoped it was my final breath, too, because I could not imagine a life without his laughter and antics.

I could not keep him alive. I could not stop the cancer. I was his mother, given one task to protect the boy I loved.

I found him on the pages of my journal, that plaid-covered book I bought at Dillard's for $8.99. I wrote while he watched *Toy Story* for the fifth time in one day while potent medicines raced inside his veins. I found myself, too.

I had not been a bad mother. I had not saved him, but I had loved him.

I still do.

~*~
Twenty-two

For Memorial Day, the cemetery grounds crew decorates the graves of war veterans with starch cloth flags on sticks. When you gaze out over the lawn and see the flags, you are thankful for those who served to protect our nation. Memorial Day holds significance for me since that was the weekend in 1996 when Daniel's pediatrician called to tell us what the hospital lab had discovered. We saw our friends in their van heading to our church picnic; our family would spend the weekend at the hospital.

Years ago, I became a collector of motivational quotes and saved them in a computer file marked "Quotes to Inspire." I pull out this file for a quick boost or to add to the quotes.

When I learned how even in his death Abraham Lincoln still inspired a nation, I included a few paragraphs in my file about the tradition his death started. Lincoln's body was transported in a coffin on a train to Springfield, Illinois, for the funeral. When the train stopped, and his coffin was displayed at various venues, people created bouquets and placed them on the coffin to honor him. Because of people's love for Lincoln, a new tradition was born—placing flowers at a grave. And, eventually, a day was set aside to honor those who had died in the Civil War. Memorial Day was once called Decoration Day because of the way people all across the United States placed flowers on the tombs of those who had died in the war.

Seated on a towel with a cup of coffee, I stretched my legs and rested my back against the oak beside Daniel's grave. Birds flitted; a butterfly pranced from grave to grave. I breathed in the calm nature provided and the solace God gave to my soul. I closed my eyes.

When I finished my coffee, I stood, ready to walk the road that circled the grounds. My goal was to walk at least two miles. My four-miles-per-day routine had vanished once Carl and my wood-engraving business picked up, and we had online orders to fulfill. The business paid the mortgage, and although I am not a creative wood type, luckily, Carl has that skill.

I walked around the cemetery three times, praying and even singing a little. When I was parallel with the Jesus statue, a car pulled up. A woman in pink sneakers got out and carried a bouquet to a grave about ten yards from me. I didn't want to be in the way of her time at this sacred place, so I stepped up my pace toward Daniel's grave. Reaching it, I resumed my earlier spot on his Thomas the Tank Engine towel. I watched the woman place the cuts of day lilies, roses, and gerberas into the built-in container. She then stood back to view her work. She needs to do this, I thought. Look at her. This is what she can do. And from watching her, I knew flowers are a tangible way to honor the dead. It is something we can do when there seems like nothing is left to be done. Americans wanted to show their love for Abe Lincoln, and flowers on the grave were a way to express sorrow. Placing flowers on the tomb is a way to give gifts to those who don't need anything from us anymore. But we, the earth's living, still need to do something lovely for them. Placing flowers on the grave is a gift we give ourselves.

I withdrew my uncertainty about flowers at the cemetery. I needed to call my Grandma Patsie and tell her I was sorry for judging her back when she took flowers to Granddad's grave at the plot in Amelia County Courthouse, Virginia. As a college student visiting her during spring and summer breaks, she'd drive us to Amelia County. She'd stop at Safeway to buy a bouquet of roses and baby's breath along the way. At the grave, she'd solemnly set the arrangement on the ground. I'd think, *He's in heaven. He's not getting those flowers. What a waste of money*. But on this day, I wanted to call to tell her I understood those flowers were her way of showing love. She would have rather hugged him, made him a ham sandwich or sliced tomatoes for his dinner. He did love those home-grown tomatoes. Her act of buying the flowers and placing them by his grave was not for him; it was for her.

I would have called my Grandma Patsie to tell her my thoughts had she still been alive.

~*~

When I visited Daniel's grave on a summer morning, there was a toy plastic police car seated on top. I took a photo and sent it along with a text to ask Rachel if she'd placed the car there. She replied she hadn't, so we called it the mystery gift. Months later, there was an addition, a red toy car. Again, Rachel had no idea where it had come from. For years a rock had been on the edge of his marker, and in time, it had lodged into the dirt by the right side. We called it a dino rock since it looked prehistoric like it had been part of some archeological dig.

Rachel and I planned to write at Daniel's Place on an October afternoon when the humidity had long disappeared. We noted the two cars upright by Daniel's name and, once more, wondered who had left them. The three stems of artificial flowers were ones Rachel had brought and stuck in the dirt, so we knew the origin of those. But the cars baffled us. Rachel was thirty-two now, and in her early twenties was diagnosed with borderline personality disorder. Learning how to navigate her mental health has been a challenge. Thankfully, she finds the grassy slopes of the cemetery a safe haven. "Like mother, like daughter," she tells me.

I'd brought beach towels, but when Rachel mentioned she had folding deck chairs in the trunk of her car, I knew what I preferred. We parked ourselves in the chairs in the northern section of the cemetery. This isolated region, the Jewish quarter of Markham Memorial, is located off the circular driveway, beyond the mausoleum. The grass was thick and soft; I removed my shoes and let my toes wiggle. We talked; there was much to share about our lives since we'd last been together. But we had come to the cemetery with the plan to write, so we had to make ourselves accountable.

"Let's write for an hour without talking," I said, and Rachel set the timer on her phone.

We entered our own thoughts and allowed for silence. But, as I read pages from my old journals, I wanted to break the tranquility and talk about the recorded events from years ago. Journals show what we once felt and thought. Reading them helps us feel relief and gratitude that we have grown in wisdom and hope.

When a chime broke into our sentences, we were relieved to be able to speak again.

"Listen to this," I said, reading from a page in a journal. "You took your gray plastic chair and Daniel's blue one here. And," I added, turning the page to another entry, "You brought stickers and covered his grave with them."

She laughed. "How old was I then?"

"Seven."

Switching from happy memories to somber ones, I said, "When I write about your dad, it's hard." I looked over a section in my manuscript I wrote after pulling details from one of my journals.

"Why is that?"

"I'd like to skip all the parts about how he spiraled. I don't want to write about it at all, but I have to include something, or readers won't understand why we divorced. Plus, I have to write that we were divorced if I want to bring Carl into the story."

"I wouldn't worry about it. Dad's not going to read your book." She smiled, and I joined her. I doubted David would read my book, should it ever get published. Once, he'd been an avid science fiction reader. But these days, whenever the kids visited him in his apartment in South Carolina, they returned saying he no longer had that desire. "Don't worry," Rachel repeated.

"Okay," I said. "I'll write enough to let readers know what happened."

We agreed to set the timer on Rachel's phone again and returned to our pens and pages. The sun lowered in the sky, the light wind rustled the nearby trees, and the graves stayed silent.

That day, I was grateful Rachel had found value in the tool of writing and was being helped by its benefits. She knows I believe the world would be better if people took the time to write. Writing is cheap therapy that heals. Writing brings clarity and calms restless minds. I suppose those two lines could be on my epitaph. If my kids select a small grave marker without much room, *Write!* will suffice.

~*~
Twenty-three

I bought sushi and watermelon slices at the grocery store, and then stopped at a convenience store a few miles from Daniel's Place. I poured some medium roast coffee into a Styrofoam cup, added the half and half from a dispenser, stirred, and took a sip. "Ugh!" I grabbed a napkin from another dispenser and spit the mouthful into it. "This is sour," I told the shop owner and then asked what he wanted me to do with the cup of coffee.

He apologized and said he'd refill the cream dispenser with fresh half and half. He took the cup from me. I proceeded to pour another cup of coffee. I saw a basket of International Delights creamers. They are the ones that need no refrigeration. I chose hazelnut, since there was no plain style. I stirred and sipped; it was good. It wasn't Starbucks coffee, but that was probably why it was only $1.39.

Daniel's Place greeted me with a layer of fog. I parked the Jeep in my customary spot. "Hi, baby," I said, as I approached his marker. Twigs and sticks lay broken around it. I did my usual mothering— brushing them away and wiping bird poop off his name with a wet towelette I keep in my purse for such occasions.

Usually serene and with an atmosphere of holiness, on that day, there was noise. Straight ahead, about fifteen geese were by the circular driveway on the other side of the cemetery.

The ruckus was not quite as noisy and furious as the beasts in *Where the Wild Things Are*, but there was enough friction to make me wonder what was going on. As I walked over towards the gaggle of feathered creatures with my camera, a few went in the opposite direction, one stopped and looked at me, and the others continued in some sort of discombobulated manner. They cackled and wobbled, and their long necks bobbed. It was like a board meeting I'd once attended at my kids' charter school; no one had a clear idea of what was happening. I kept taking photos of the geese, because I had never seen them at the cemetery before. When I realized I had probably taken too many pictures, I left them and walked to the Jeep to get my pen, pad, and towel. I opened the Jeep door and reached for my bag, and that was when it happened. There was a sound unlike I'd ever heard before that riveted the entire cemetery. The noise, with raucous momentum, was caused by those feathered birds who had taken off into the sky. As they flew high above me in a formatted line, they called out to each other. I had to get a picture, but when I pointed and aimed, the geese were too far into the sky, just little specks dotting the gray canvas, just the way helium balloons get after they've been released.

I wondered how all those geese that had seemed so confused just minutes before suddenly flew in sync with harmony, purpose, and direction. Which one had given the sign that it was time to take off? Had one of them lifted a foot, indicating that the chaos had to end? A wink? Can geese wink? How had such a motley crew taken off in such a glorious formation?

One moment they were confused. They had no idea where they were, what they wanted, or whether they would live or die, and the next, they were the definition of sublime awe. They had transformed from squawking whiners into graceful art.

When I looked at the photo on my camera, they were barely recognizable. I doubted anyone could tell if they were geese or blobs. But I had wanted to capture them. I wanted to have them as part of my life. I knew what it's like to be confused, to wonder, to doubt, to fear, and to eventually soar. Soar with purpose. Before the flight, these geese appeared like newly-bereaved parents.

I knew little about Canadian geese, except for their ability to stop traffic when crossing the street near a strip mall. But after watching them cohesively fly together from the cemetery, I wanted to know more. That's when I found the website BirdEden and was grateful for those who have taken it upon themselves to study Canadian geese. The V shape is aerodynamic, and the birds in the back don't have to work as hard because of the air current created by those in the front of the line. Since the front flyer has to work the hardest, he gets a break. Others take turns. When the lead feathered aviator grows weary, he drops to the back of the group, and the next bird gets a go at being the front flyer. This made me nod and smile, but what I found most amusing was these geese care for each other. When one of them gets sick or old, the healthy younger crowd will stay behind and sit with the weak or elderly. Learning this has endeared me to geese. Who would have thought these noisy creatures that will stop traffic when drivers are in a hurry to get somewhere would stay behind to assist a fellow goose in need?

God of all creation, you marvel me. My creativity pales in comparison to a star-studded night, a sunset, and geese in flight.

~*~

Canadian Academy, my high school in Kobe, Japan, where I attended for four years, had a surprise for me. Henry, the alumni director, invited me to be the school's author-in-residence for a week. I had never played the lottery, but I had hit the jackpot. Returning to Japan after twenty-eight years was remarkable; eating authentic *oyakodomburi*, *tempura*, *soba*, and *takoyaki*—all my comfort foods—was enjoyable. However, whenever I recall the trip, what stands out most is being left behind in Hiroshima during a field trip. After a Shinkansen ride and ferry rides to and from the island of Miyajima, a chartered bus took the thirty students,

127

five chaperones, the alumni director, and me to the Hiroshima Peace Museum. Inside the museum, students breezed through the artifacts, photos, and testimonies of the bomb dropped on the town. As I meandered through, I got lost in the history.

When I left the museum and walked outside, I didn't see anyone from our group. Where were they? I spent the next hours walking the premises, hoping to see a familiar face. It was a rainy January day, and the grounds were covered in puddles; I am sure I stepped in all of them. As I walked, I was both saddened and disgusted no one had come to find me.

Finally, after circling and muttering (perhaps I'm part goose), I realized no one would find me. I had to venture away from the park and the designated meeting area, where no one from the group was anymore, and find my own way. While geese don't leave any feathered friend behind, that is not how humans act. I eventually got a street car and bullet train back to Kobe. On the train, I used my journal to record my angry feelings. Hours later back in my hotel room, I wrote deep into the night and early morning. I suppose I am that female who wants to be rescued and wants God to whisk me out of my troubles. He provides a path for me to walk and promises to never leave me, but there are times when I wish he would carry me into the sky, even on the back of a Canadian goose, so I don't have to do the hard work of walking on my own.

~*~

The geese flew with their high-decibel sounds, and I watched until they were but a dot in the gray sky. I waved even though they could not see me and then laughed. *I just met geese from Canada.* They had seemed discombobulated until they'd joined together and knew their purpose. Calling out to them, I said, "Cackle, go, fly, soar. And stay warm, that's the reason you have traveled from the north to the south."

As I walked around the pavement with my convenience store coffee, I thought of the balloons we'd released over the years and the friends who had joined us for birthday picnics. I sang a few lines of *Jesus Loves Me* because Daniel had sung that, and I also knew the love of Jesus sustained me, even though I wanted to, at first, push Jesus, his Father, and the Holy Spirit aside.

Solomon's grave greeted me once again. His epitaph was God's reminder to stay focused on what matters so that at the end of life I could join in the sentiment: *I have finished my course, I have kept the faith.*

From Solomon's resting spot I crossed the grass to the pavement and walked briskly around the premises. Doubt that I could ever finish a book because of the fear my pain might be misunderstood crept around the corner. Would I be judged? Doubt stood, although I was sure I was the only one who could see him. I walked faster, and as I did, I said, "No fear. Not today."

It doesn't have to be perfect, said Breezy. *It just has to be real.* And then she added in her best Southern accent, *Just get 'er done. Please.*

I spread Daniel's Thomas the Tank Engine towel under the oak and placed my coffee, sushi, and watermelon slices on a level section of the grass. I sat, stretched my legs, and opened my notebook. I picked out the biggest piece of watermelon and took a bite. Smiling at my son's tiny remembrance square, I thought of the first time I had stood beside it. That day I had doubted I'd ever be able to soar again.

~*~
Twenty-four

Life is precious. The hospital staff repeated those words as I agonized over Daniel losing his.
Life *is* precious. The desire to live and protect our loved ones is natural, too. But according to the Bible, so is looking forward to the life hereafter.

At any cemetery, not just Daniel's Place, I feel I've taken a dozen steps into heaven. My friend Beth told me a cemetery is the invisible church—those already in heaven—and the rest of us Christians still fighting the fight and finishing our course are part of the visible church. The Apostle Paul put it so well in the fourth chapter of II Corinthians, telling us not to lose heart when we feel weighed down and weary because each moment of feeling worn is an opportunity to lean against Jesus and look to what is to come. It's a mystery what heaven is exactly like. I've been

131

known to ask, "What do you do there?" The answers I hear are, we'll rule and reign with Jesus. I think of all the natural beauty God created, beauty I get to see every spring, and am certain that heaven's beauty is more glorious. The sunflowers are brighter there than those grown in earth's soil; the peacock orchids in my garden are more vibrant in eternity. Once during a bone scan, Daniel created a song: "Heaven, heaven, heaven is a good place to stay." At the time, I cringed. Why would he make up a song like that? But now, the memory gives me peace.

I'm grateful that this life, as precious as it is on earth, is not all we were created for. Thank you, Jesus, for the glory that will be mine one day. No more goodbyes at our forever home, no more tears, no more doubt. Face to face with our King of kings, our Lord of lords, our faith will be eternally perfect.

~*~

How peculiar it is that I call Daniel's Place *the simple quiet* because it isn't without sound. Standing by the oak that shades Daniel's grave, when you look over the lush lawn and past the road leading to Markham Memorial Gardens, the traffic from I-40 is visible. You also hear it. If you concentrate on the sounds of vehicle engines, that is all you hear. But when I focus on the birds and the wind and scan the sky for that cemetery hawk, the sound of vehicles tunes out.

This is how I'd like to live. There is noise at the grocery store, post office, and other places I frequent. Then there's the TV, the phone ringing, and videos on YouTube. Sometimes the clamor of living is loud, and I get obsessed with listening to it. I don't hear God's whisper. I'm not still enough to know that he is God.

I come to the grave to be part of tranquility. Absorbed in my writing or pondering, the interstate traffic fades. I only hear it again when I need to head home and return to my other life. Then I join the fray, hoping to keep God's voice nearby, hoping I can apply the lessons of the cemetery's classroom to every part of living.

~*~

Author's Note

This memoir was written with the help of journals, letters, and photos. Some of the names have been changed.

~*~

About the Author

Alice J. Wisler has been an advocate for writing ever since the death of Daniel, her four-year-old son, in 1997. She speaks on the benefits of writing through sorrow on her podcast and at workshops and conferences across the country. She has written numerous articles for bereavement publications, and is the author of six novels, two were Christy Award finalists. Her devotional, *Getting Out of Bed in the Morning: Reflections of Comfort in Heartache* (Leafwood Publishers), is for those wanting to seek God in the midst of sorrow and suffering. Read more at her website: http://www.alicewisler.com.